Freshwater Marshes
Ecology and Wildlife Management

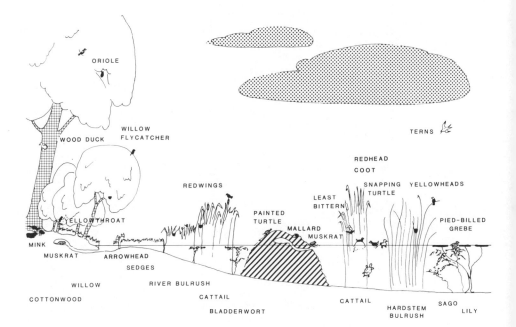

ORIOLE

WILLOW FLYCATCHER

WOOD DUCK

TERNS

REDHEAD
COOT

SNAPPING TURTLE   YELLOWHEADS

REDWINGS

LEAST BITTERN

PAINTED TURTLE

YELLOWTHROAT

MALLARD
MUSKRAT

PIED-BILLED GREBE

MINK

MUSKRAT   ARROWHEAD

SEDGES

WILLOW   RIVER BULRUSH

COTTONWOOD   CATTAIL

BLADDERWORT

CATTAIL

HARDSTEM BULRUSH

SAGO

LILY

Wildlife Habitats

Milton W. Weller, Series Editor

Freshwater Marshes

Ecology and Wildlife Management

Second Edition

MILTON W. WELLER

University of Minnesota Press □ Minneapolis

The John K. Fesler Memorial Fund provided
assistance in the publication of this volume, for which
the University of Minnesota Press is grateful.

Published by the University of Minnesota Press
2037 University Avenue Southeast, Minneapolis MN 55414.
Published simultaneously in Canada
by Fitzhenry & Whiteside Limited, Markham.
Printed in the United States of America.

Library of Congress Cataloging-in-Publication Data

Weller, Milton Webster.
   Freshwater marshes.

   (Wildlife habitats)
   Bibliography: p.
   Includes index.
   1. Marsh ecology. 2. Freshwater ecology.
3. Wildlife management. 4. Wetland conservation.
I. Title. II. Series.
QH541.M3W44   1987   574.5'26325   87-11364
ISBN 0-8166-1549-7
ISBN 0-8166-1550-0 (pbk.)

To my wife, Doris

Preface

This little book on marshes and marsh wildlife is intended mainly to provide a general introduction for interested laypersons, students, and professionals in other fields. Experienced marsh specialists may find some of the viewpoints, data, or ideas given here worth considering, but the text has not been prepared at a highly technical level. Because of the current interest in the wildlife of marshes and in the conservation of natural areas as part of our national heritage, I have put together some general information about marshes and about some of the problems involved in their preservation.

Marshes have always been important to hunters and trappers, who in turn have been influential in their preservation. Fishermen too now recognize the values of marshes as spawning and rearing areas, and some have become interested in their management. Moreover, it is becoming increasingly obvious that marshes play crucial roles in water quality, water retention, enhancement of water tables, erosion control, and soil and nutrient trapping, and are valuable in providing "greenspace." Recent environmental protection laws have induced interest where it was not already present, and lawyers, sociologists, economists, consulting firms, developers, and land managers of all kinds are concerned about wetland evaluation and protection as they have never been before.

Anyone who tackles a task of this kind does so with certain biases. So that you fully understand the reasons for some of these emphases, you should know that my major research and experience in North America have been with the birds and some mammals and plants of (a) glacially formed "pothole" marshes in the prairies of Iowa, Manitoba, the Dakotas, and Minnesota; (b) lakeshore marshes such as the Delta Marsh of Lake Manitoba; (c) a Great Basin marsh in Utah; (d) the unique permafrost basins of the Alaskan Arctic Coastal Plain; and (e) coastal fresh and salt marshes in Texas. In addition to my personal involvements, I have tried to broaden the scope of the book to subjects that I consider vital to an understanding of the issue. However, those readers interested particularly in plants or invertebrates may find my tendency to consider these as nest substrates or food to be misleading. Nevertheless, I hope the non-specialist still will be able to gain here an increased appreciation of the various components of the marsh, their values and interrelations, and the conflict between man and wetlands. But because of my own interest and experience, the emphasis is on the wildlife of marshes, how they interact, the potential of and procedures for management of marshes for wildlife, and the effects of natural forces on the functioning of this unique system.

Separating the components of the marsh will, I hope, help readers to appreciate what a marsh is, what's in it, and how it operates, without oversimplification. Ultimately, the reader must synthesize these components, for understanding a marsh is understanding a concept of a complex interacting, dynamic ecological system *(ecosystem)*[153] that has a physical *form* or *structure*, interactions of members of a single *population* of a *species,* diverse relationships of various species of plants and animals living together as a *community,* and a flow of nutrients (= energy) through the community that allows the system to function.

This book may produce mental conflict for some readers because it considers both the pristine and the manipulated, the economically tangible and the esoteric, the hunted and the non-hunted, and the conflict of wildlife with man as well as the benefits of wildlife to man. Management philosophies and approaches may be the most difficult to accept, but they must be viewed objectively in relation to the current state of the environment. I am the first to encourage managers to leave well enough alone, but marshes can profit by human management—if the tools of management are natural and effective, and the products are acceptable to society.

Attitudes toward marshes and marsh conservation vary dramatically. At one end of the scale is the drain, fill, and build-over syndrome; at the other end is the concept of preserving intact. Neither may be totally feasible in today's society, but perhaps the reader will be able to evaluate alternatives more objectively after reading this book. Solutions are not provided for all of the problems raised, nor are they likely to come easily, but a general knowledge and appreciation of the pros and cons will enable more effective decision-making by man, the controller of so many natural systems. If in the judgment of most of mankind, marshes are to be replaced by concrete, so it will be—but the world will not be the better for it.

Acknowledgments

Many people have influenced my thinking on marshes and have gone out of their way to help me to understand them better. Among the most noteworthy are William H. Elder (University of Missouri), Peter Ward and H. Albert Hochbaum (Delta Waterfowl Research Station), the late Paul L. Errington (Iowa State University), Leigh Fredrickson (University of Missouri), David Trauger (U. S. Fish and Wildlife Service), and David Voigts (Florida Power Corp.).

My research on marshes has been financed directly or indirectly by various organizations at various times in my career: the University of Missouri, the Delta Waterfowl Research Station, Iowa State University, the Iowa Conservation Commission, the U. S. Fish and Wildlife Service, the University of Minnesota, and Texas A & M University. I am indebted to many individuals in these organizations for their interest and assistance.

Table of Contents

PREFACE vii

ACKNOWLEDGMENTS xi

Chapter 1. INTRODUCTION 3

Chapter 2. MARSH BASINS,
HYDROLOGY, AND DIVERSITY 7
Basin Formation via Physical Forces 7
Biological Influences 11
Hydrology 11
Classification 13
Wetland Diversity 17

Chapter 3. SUBSTRATE AND
VEGETATION STRUCTURE 18
Substrate 18
Water Depth Influences on Plants 18
Plant Life-Forms 20
Marsh Islands, Edge, and Layers 23

Chapter 4. THE MARSH AS A SYSTEM 25
Food Chains and Webs 26
Nutrients 28

Chapter 5. SOME ASPECTS OF MARSH COMMUNITIES 31
Animal Adaptations 31

Competition and Resource Segregation   32
Social Relationships   33
Sounds of the Marsh   34
The Marsh Edge   35

Chapter 6.   DOMINANT ANIMALS 36
Birds   36
Mammals   41
Fish   44
Amphibians   45
Reptiles   46
Invertebrates   47

Chapter 7.   HABITAT DYNAMICS 51
Seasonality and Wildlife Responses to It   51
Succession and Other Changes   53
  Short-Term Vegetational Changes   56
  Muskrat Populations   58
  Impact of Vegetation Change
    on Bird Populations   62
The Importance of Food Resources   67
The Importance of Instability   70

Chapter 8.   MANAGEMENT AND RESTORATION 71
Philosophical Considerations   71
Acquisition of Wetlands   73
Natural Methods: Water Level Regulation   74
Natural Methods: Herbivores and
  Other Vegetation Management   77
Artificial Methods   78
New Marshes from Old: Marsh Restoration   81
Marshes Where They Were Not   82
Birds Versus Fish   82
The Coming of the Carp and Other Exotics   83
The Limits of Management   84

Chapter 9.   MARSHES AND MAN 88
Loss of Marshes—The Good and Bad   88
Valuating and Evaluating Marshes   90
Negative Aspects of Marshes   93
Water Level Modification   95

Water Level Stability 98
Marshes for Water Purification and Energy 100
Wildlife Users—The Watchers 101
Wildlife Users—The Takers 102
Endangered Species and Endangered Habitats 103
Science 104

Chapter 10. MARSHES FOR THE FUTURE 107
The Human Need for Water 107
Wetlands in Conflict 108
Conservation Goals and Policies 110

EPILOGUE 110

APPENDIX A. Some Elementary
Marsh Study Techniques 113

APPENDIX B. Managing Duck
Hunting or Furbearer Areas 119

APPENDIX C. Scientific Names
of Plants and Animals Mentioned in the Text 122

APPENDIX D. Glossary of
Terms Used in the Text 124

REFERENCES 133

INDEX 145

Freshwater Marshes
Ecology and Wildlife Management

CHAPTER 1
Introduction

Any undisturbed low spot that will hold water over soil forms a suitable basin for the invasion of water-tolerant, rooted, perennial, soft-stemmed plants such as sedges, cattail, and bulrush. This semiaquatic plant community is a marsh and forms diverse habitats for many types of animals. Standing water is not always present, as organic soils may hold sufficient water to promote germination and sustain the growth of emergent hydrophytes. In some cases, hydrophytes may be missing for a period of time, but the soils are characteristic of those developed under water.[42] Some authors now speak of marshes as "emergent" wetlands, which designation helps to separate them from wooded swamps, where water-tolerant trees or shrubs are dominant, or moss-lichen bogs, where shorter and more fragile semiaquatic plants grow. Although we often speak of a marsh as a discrete entity, and this kind of marsh is the easier concept to identify and discuss, the term "marsh" also is applied to typical marsh vegetation that may be distributed as patches or strips along the shallow edges of lakes, seashores or rivers.

Because of my own experience, I have chosen most of the examples here from freshwater marshes of the glaciated grasslands of the Midwest, which are typical of those at mid-latitudes of the world where climatic seasons are dramatic. Emergent marshes may occur at any latitude, but they are poorly developed at very high latitudes (Arctic or Antarctic) because of the permafrost, cold, and reduced productivity of such areas; and in wet tropical forests, such marshes may be replaced by shrub or tree swamps. It is the mid-latitude marshes that are renowned for their rich

The prairie marsh; the addition of water and the subtle diversity of color and texture to the gently rolling grassland.

productivity both in terms of plant quantity (*biomass*) and the myriads of insects and waterbirds that have attracted man's attention. This type of marsh is one of the most productive of all systems on earth in terms of capturing and converting sunlight to stored energy.[169] Although I focus here on inland systems, many of the concepts and principles described are in evidence along the coasts where isolated freshwater marshes may be common and where even tidal marshes may be fresh or nearly fresh as runoff from the uplands is held back by the sea. Moreover, brackish or even saline marshes in estuaries and lagoonal areas may show similar structural and biological patterns.

Each marsh is a complex community of living organisms interacting with their physical environment. The study of such communities is still in its infancy, but the products of the research have broad implications for the comprehension of natural systems in relation to man. Work on a bog-lake and on coastal tidal marshes has been especially important in understanding energy flow in the ecological system.[153] Work on coastal marshes has enhanced our knowledge of how marshes serve as nutrient traps that then enrich the adjacent ecosystem, the ocean.[48, 206] Studies of freshwater marshes have focused more on the production of wildlife from such marshes, the man-made and natural habitat changes that influence[23, 155] wildlife use and diversity, and the social systems within and between species.[154, 231] But most of the work on both freshwater and marine systems has been observational rather than experimental, so that replicated experiments have been rare.

To facilitate a grasp of some terminology and various of the scientific perspectives, it may be useful to list the kinds of scientists who have studied marshes and how their diverse interests and approaches contribute to the understanding of this complex system: Formation of marshes usually involves land form, so *geologists* (specifically geomorphologists) concerned with glaciers, rivers, soil movement, and other dynamic physical forces clarify processes and actions by which basins are formed. *Climatologists* are concerned mainly about the weather-related phenomena such as rain, snow, and storms that influence marsh water levels. *Hydrologists* study the flow and accumulation of water in basins and matters pertaining to regulation of water levels. The study of water in such basins, and particularly the aquatic life of freshwater, is done by *limnologists*. Fortunately, a number of *botanists* interested in marsh and aquatic plants have written useful guide books,[65, 94, 146] as well as done detailed work on plant populations and nutrient dynamics in plants. Work by *ornithologists* on the birds of marshes and of *mammalogists* on the mammals have provided data on the biology and behavior of various species, on *species richness* (i.e. the number of different species), and *species diversity* (species richness mathematically related to population size of each species). Few *ichthyologists* have studied the fishes of marshes, however, and more studies by *herpetologists* on the amphibians (frogs, salamanders, toads) or reptiles (snakes, alligators) of wetlands also are needed. *Entomologists* have done a great deal more work, but there is so much more to do, because insects are the most numerous group in terms of species richness or population size. Other *invertebrate zoologists* concentrate on mollusks, crustaceans, protozoans and other phyla or classes of animals that lack backbones. *Ecologists* have concerned themselves mainly with the interrelationships of species, the evolution of communities of naturally associated species, and the energy relationships by which the *ecosystem* functions. *Wildlife biologists* have studied marshes most, because the production of wildlife is so commonly dependent on marshes. This review is based mainly on the ideas and data of such scientists; our knowledge of wetlands is much farther along because of their fascination for marshes or their need to resolve some practical problem.

Key words, usually defined by logical inference, are in italics. For readers who wish to explore some of these ideas in greater detail, or to interpret findings for themselves, general references are listed alphabetically in the back of the book and are cited numerically in the text. Recent additions to the references are cited by number and letter, e.g., 118a, 11b. Some suggestions for simple studies of marshes and their biota are given in Appendix A. For those hunters and trappers who would like to apply some of the general marsh management concepts described in the text, Appendix B gives some suggestions. Scientific names of plants and animals are listed in Appendix C, and a glossary of terms as used by wildlife biologists and wetland ecologists is given in Appendix D.

CHAPTER 2
Marsh Basins, Hydrology, and Diversity

Marshes are formed in any basin that will hold water long enough for the germination and survival of semiaquatic or aquatic plants. Basins probably hold water poorly when they are new, unless they are created in fine silt or clay that seals easily, but buildup of organic matter helps to fill the many pores. Eventually, basins collect groundwater, rainfall, snowmelt, or floodwater from watershed, river, or lake.

Basin Formation via Physical Forces

Most wetland basins are land forms created by tectonic action such as mountain building, by water movement, glacier or other ice action, [168] soil slippage,[221] or even by meteorites. Depending on local climatic conditions, extensive geographic regions may be characterized by one wetland type. The distribution of water-loving ducks is a good measure of both the distribution and productivity of important wetland zones (Fig. 1).[63, 107]

Glacial action, especially sheet glaciers of the Pleistocene epoch, formed the massive Prairie Pothole Region of the North Central United States and western prairie Canada. This area once covered some three hundred thousand square miles and probably was one of the richest wetland regions in the entire world because of the abundance of lakes, marshes, and smaller wetlands located in rich soils with a warm summer climate. The areas of greatest pothole abun-

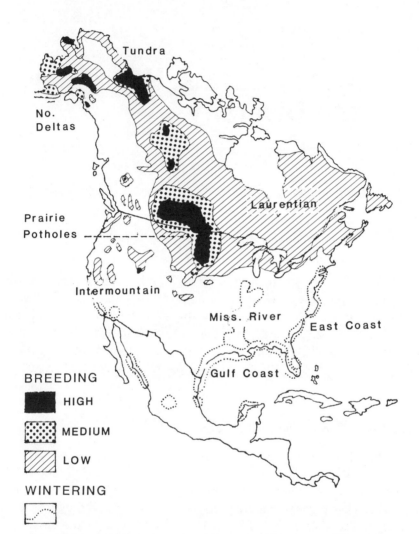

Figure 1. *General pattern of duck distribution in North America during summer breeding (pattern) and wintering (dots) serves as an index to the general distribution of various types of wetlands.*[107] *Major breeding areas are in the glacially formed Prairie Pothole Region, in the coastal tundra and riverine marshes of Alaska and Canada, and in the western intermountain and Great Basin marshes. Lesser numbers occur in the deep and sterile lakes of the Laurentian Shield of Canada. Major wintering areas are in coastal lagoons and bays and estuaries of southern and eastern coasts, and along river oxbows and delta marshes of the Mississippi River, as well as in western basin marshes.*

dance are moraines of undulating glacial till. Once these sand and gravel basins were sealed with finer silts, water retention created suitable depths that induced growth of aquatic plants. Moraines of various types also influence stream and river flowages, with a resultant formation of major lakes in some cases and smaller, marshy basins in others. The ancient glacial Lake Agassiz of the North Central Region and southern Canada left undulations from old shorelines and underwater deposits. Extensive marshes and bogs have formed in these basins within the former lake bottom.

Intermountain depressions often are quite deep and, where water is abundant, lakes rather than marshes form. These depressions may be filled by eroded uplands to create more shallow, marshy basins, or they may dry out because of arid conditions. Marshes and meandering streams may be formed on the flats. Water levels in intermountain valleys of the western United States often have snow as their chief source, so levels may vary drastically from the spring snowmelt period to late summer when water has evaporated.[51] Moreover, year-to-year fluctuation in snowfall in mountains quite some distance away may influence levels in the basin. Where spring rains are prominent, similar seasonal water patterns result.

Gravel, sand, and soil deposited along the shore of major lakes by either wave or ice action create a marginal basin that traps water moving from the surrounding watershed. The resultant marsh differs little from other marshes except that periodic reflooding from the lake may recharge the nutrients of both the marsh and the lake areas —changing the chemical composition of the water and washing nutrients from the richer marsh system into the larger water body. The productivity of such areas is influenced by the degree and rate of nutrient exchange between the systems. Vast marshes of this type along the Great Lakes, the huge prairie lakes of Manitoba (such as Lakes Manitoba, Winnipeg, and Winnipegosis) not only are major waterfowl producers[90] but strongly influence the quality of fishery resources in those lakes. A comparable but even more dynamic system occurs in coastal marshes, where tides may flush the vegetation daily and enrich adjacent shallow marine areas.[48]

Rivers form marshes indirectly through their meanders as they cut new channels and abandon old courses. Oxbow lakes result, and siltation eventually produces oxbow marshes that tend to become progressively more shallow and less lakelike. Because of their drainage of large areas, such marshes may be extremely rich, but the character of their plant and animal species often is influenced by annual flooding and the resultant siltation. Although such flooding resupplies nutrients annually, species of perennial plants that will not tolerate periodic flooding and drying are reduced or eliminated. Plants that are well adapted to this unstable system, such as annuals or perennials that establish easily by seed, are highly productive and become dominants. Intrusions of silt eventually may fill in these basins, especially where fast-moving flood water is slowed. Aquatic plants stressed by such silt often die out, and terrestrial flora and fauna gradually invade. The plant production resulting from these areas is washed seaward whenever floods fill the oxbow, and marsh and river are contiguous.

Riverine marshes also are found where major streams form deltas or spread out as braided streams on extensive flood plains. Marshland of the Mississippi River Delta represents this type of marsh, and similar extensive riverine marshes occur elsewhere in the world. In Iraq, the delta marsh system of the Tigris and Euphrates rivers covers thousands of square miles and is the home of an entire human culture that lives in and depends on the marsh for food and housing.[136]

In arid western intermountain regions such as the Great Basin, major rivers pour into sumps, where no drainages exist and where water levels are decreased by evaporation and by plant transpiration. Such systems become highly alkaline or saline, such as Malheur Lake in Oregon[50] or the Great Salt Lake of Utah.[39] Concentrations of salts eventually may reach a stage where few plants or animals can adapt.

In Arctic and alpine areas, frost action segregates rock and soil particles of various sizes and shifts them in such a way that "polygonal earth" patterns are formed. Those with low centers become basins that capture snowmelt.[20] In the Arctic coastal tundra, characterized by permanently frozen (permafrost) shallow organic soils, sun-heating (insolation) of snowmelt water results in the formation of basins by the thawing of the ice substrate. Further warming of the water in the pool thaws the substrate until an equilibrium is reached between the temperature of the sun-heated water and the chill of the permafrost basin underneath.

Biological Influences

The major biological influence in marshes is the dense growth of diverse plants that capture sunlight and build plant biomass, slow water movement, seal basins, induce settling of particulate matter from the water, and protect extensive areas from wind action. These actions generally reduce basin depth via deposition of peaty organic materials. Depending on the slope of the land, water-retaining mechanisms of plants aid in building their own wetland, such as occurs in the extensive sedge meadows and blanket bogs of northern forest areas.

Depressions of various sizes are created by crayfish, muskrats, alligators, seals, elephants, and other animals, in various geographic areas of the world. These biological forces hardly create marshes, but they deepen small areas of a marsh and may strongly influence the rate at which the bottom peat layer builds up and where plants are distributed. Indirectly, through the action of carp and muskrats (in combination with waves and ice), large areas of plants may float to the surface, carrying soil with them in the rootstocks. Such actions aid in deepening marsh basins, but also create turbid water. These animals are important influences on wetlands though not the causative agent forming major aquatic systems.

The major animal builder of wetlands is the beaver, but in most cases ponds or reservoirs are created rather than marshes.[17] Nonetheless, they provide similar kinds of habitat in an otherwise streamlike environment. Typically, these ponds have rather abrupt shores but sedges and, occasionally, broad-leaved cattail are found in the upper reaches. Water lilies and other pad-plants are common in the deeper water.

Hydrology

One usually assumes that water in marshes is a product of direct rainfall, snowfall, or runoff from adjacent slopes, or at most the overflow of rivers in riverine marshes. But hydrologists and ecologists, though they have only scratched the surface in the study of wetlands, have found much more diverse patterns. In fact, there are classification systems for wetlands in which water source, rate of flow, and relationship to ground water are major criteria.

Emergent marshes may have water levels that are not influenced by the deep ground water table but are in "sealed" or "perched" basins above the level of that table, which in part explains their highly variable water levels. But extensive wetland areas such as the Prairie Potholes may have water levels that reflect the water table and contribute to it. Especially when marsh water levels are high, seepage from marshes into the ground water occurs mostly at the margins. For this reason, seepage losses are greatest where wetland shoreline is largest in proportion to the water volume.[140] In several areas where the seepage into the ground level has been calculated, it tends to be less than 20 percent of the total volume of water per season, but that amount can be a major contribution to the water-shed and to water quality.[2, 52] Subsurface water flow may intersect and even interconnect potholes.[189] This water table can slope into or away from a pothole, creating a "discharge" if it slopes into a pond, and a draining "recharge" if it slopes away from the pond. In some situations, this creates a flow-through of water, but much can happen to water while in the wetland. Considerable water is lost owing to evaporation, and plant transpiration can be even more significant. In fact, transpiration loss often exceeds that due to evaporation—and is greater with tall than with short emergent plants. Because both occur during the summer, the combined loss of water through evaporation and transpiration was 2.5 feet in some North Dakota potholes, far exceeding annual rainfall (1.0 feet).[52] Thus, runoff was essential for maintenance of the water level, and snowfall, early spring rains, and carryover were essential for maintenance of levels under dry conditions. A slight modification of these water supplies shifts the prairie potholes to "wet" or "dry" cycles in a very short time. Those areas with water high in dissolved salts that also have high summer evaporation become alkaline (sulfate) or saline (chloride) wetlands, with a corresponding change in vegetation and animal life.[195] Variation in flow-through rates gradually modifies the water chemistry of the area and, eventually, the emergent vegetation, so that flushing with fresh water is a regular management practice in western[39] and coastal marshes.[36]

It should become obvious from these generalizations, which un-doubtedly vary by wetland and region, that wetlands are vital to the continental water regime. They filter water as it moves to streams and influence the rate of flow (especially during storms); they also

Large Type V open wetland dissected by a county road in North Dakota. Drainage into the wetland is increased by the road surface and the ditch formation. Salts from winter ice removal undoubtedly contaminate the water.

may act as storage basins during floods.[145] At some times of year (especially spring), they may increase the flow rate of streams that draw their water from watersheds rich in wetlands, whereas such basins may hold water in dry periods (late summer) and reduce stream flow.[151] Wetlands have a strong influence on water quality since sediments (as much as 80 percent) and heavy metals are deposited, and nitrogen, phosphorus, and other nutrients are extracted and modified by cycling within the marsh system.[102]

Some wetlands actually may draw water from lower levels by capillary action in the organic substrate. In a few cases, wetland plant associations form on hillsides where ground water discharges, so that moss, sedges, cattail, and even reed can be seen in patches on otherwise dry road cuts or hillsides.

Classification

Wildlife biologists and other wetland scientists have devised a number of systems for use in surveying marshes and their wildlife.[20, 42, 43, 75, 97, 134, 142] Three major ones currently are in use, including a new broad-based system devised for extensive mapping.[42] Shaw and Fredine[186] (Table

Table 2.1. A Partial Comparison of Two Wetland Classification Systems

Shaw and Fredine— 1956 Types	Stewart and Kantrud— 1971 Classes	Major Identifying Vegetation Type
1. Seasonally flooded basins or flats	I. Ephemeral ponds	Wet prairie grasses or annual weeds
2. Inland Fresh Meadows	II. Temporary ponds	Meadow sedges, rushes, grasses, and broadleafs
3. Inland Shallow Fresh Marshes	III. Seasonal ponds and lakes	Water-loving grasses and sedges, smartweeds, burreed
4. Inland Deep Fresh Marshes	IV. Semipermanent ponds and lakes	Cattail, hardstem bulrush, submergent pondweeds
5. Inland Open Fresh Water	V. Permanent ponds and lakes	Type IV emergents as a rim
10. Inland Saline Marshes	VI. Alkali ponds and lakes	Alkali bulrush, wigeon grass

2.1) categorized marsh and other wetland areas of the United States in a system that has become the legal basis for decisions on wetlands, known colloquially as "Circular 39" of the U.S. Fish and Wildlife Service. Water depths and periodicity of water were emphasized in this work as an influence on the vegetation that typically develops under those water regimes. Hence, a vegetation type was inferred that we commonly use in referring to plant zones: deep marsh, shallow marsh, and so forth. Stewart and Kantrud[194] (Table 2.1), working mainly in the North Dakota glaciated prairie wetlands, emphasized the relative permanence of the wetlands in the class names, but made more extensive analysis of the vegetation cover type by depth zone, as well as the changes in vegetation characteristic of the area and the wetland class. Table 2.1 shows both systems, which are reasonably comparable except for inland saline or alkaline areas, which we will not treat here in detail. Other types these researchers described include shrub swamps, wooded swamps, acid bogs, alkaline bogs (fens), and coastal wetlands.

Any classification system involves artificially dividing up what is really a continuum; hence, some wetlands will seem to fall between any two categories and may be judged differently by different classifiers. In most cases, this apparent discrepancy is probably not serious, and any one person will be fairly consistent in using a system. As we shall see, these types of wetland differ in their attractiveness to various groups of birds and other wildlife. Their distribution varies regionally as to animal associations. But more important, we shall see that depending on the criteria used, one wetland can at various stages, in even a few years of time, functionally span several of these types. Normally, however, the vegetative character of the wetland results from long-term means of water depths that produce vegetation identifiable regardless of temporary water conditions. Stewart and Kantrud resolved this classification problem by using the mean vegetation type as the class but indicating the "phase" of the wetland in relation to water levels, such as *drawdown phase*, *emergent phase*, *open-water phase*, and so on.

Because of the interest and involvement of various agencies and interest groups, wetland classification systems have become still more complex and applicable to various situations and degrees of refinement. It is hoped that the newest hierarchical system (a graded series from general to identifying specifics) will be usable by geologists, limnologists, botanists, and wildlife biologists.[42] This new system covers all wetlands so it first groups them according to general characteristics, using established scientific terms that avoid the confusion of local variation in common names. There are five major groups called Systems: Marine (only the subtidal or intertidal zones at the edge of the sea are included as wetlands), Lacustrine (shallow fresh lakes), Estuarine (brackish rather than saline coastal wetlands), Palustrine (literally "marshlike" but it includes shrub and forested swamps as well), and Riverine (wetlands within rivers rather than along them). Within all of these Systems (except Palustrine) are Subsystems (such as subtidal or littoral), and all have a third (lesser) hierarchical level termed Class. The Classes include prominent features that aid in identification such as aquatic plant bed, emergents, rock bottom, etc. Subclasses then point out characteristics shared by many wetland in the class such as Persistent (dead plant material that survives into the next season) or Nonpersistent (decomposes rapidly). A Dominance type may be used to list characteristic plant species, and other special modifiers denote water regimes, chemistry, human construction, or modification.[42] An example of a freshwater marsh using this hierarchical system is as follows:

>   System = Palustrine (marshlike)
>   Class = Emergent Wetland (versus forested, shrub, etc.)
>   Subclass = Persistent (emergent plants, versus nonpersistent)
>   Dominance Type = Cattail (for example)

Small temporary (Type II) wetland in early summer that was plowed nearly to the edge. Although too little upland remains for nesting, pairs of ducks may find isolation and food there in spring, and shorebirds find them useful during spring or fall migration.

Whether this system will replace older systems for wildlife classification is yet to be determined, but it tends to serve a broader audience and probably will function for different purposes as well.

To date, classification systems have been used more for censusing wetlands than for wildlife surveys, but several waterfowl and waterbird surveys have been made with the use of this system. These studies show associations of certain bird groups with certain wetland types.[20, 196, 197] Such data not only help us to assess what is present, but also allow us to predict what would happen if we intentionally change wetlands from one type to another.

Wetland Diversity

Because of the dominance of physical-geological forces that are responsible for the formation of most wetland basins, multiple wetlands usually are formed over a large area during a geologic period. Often, these same forces created wetlands of different depths, sizes, and intermarsh spacing in a general area. However, marsh habitat diversity differs from region to region, so that extensive areas may be dominated by shallow marshes or open lakes that influence the nature of their attractiveness to wildlife (and to people). The association of several small wetlands of the Type II (temporary) or Type III (seasonal) around a large body of water provides the greatest diversity or heterogeneity in a complex or cluster that can serve a variety of birds and other wildlife.[66, 160, 224] This diversity produced by clusters of wetlands will gain importance as we examine habitat use by various species of wildlife. It is important that we maintain this diversity of land forms and vegetative types in a natural state and with a balance characteristic of what existed in pristine times.

Diversity of wetland types and sizes is especially attractive to many marsh birds and probably is required to attract species with large home ranges. This "island" of natural wetlands in the midst of intensively farmed areas consists of about 400 acres, probably sufficient here in size because of the attractiveness of the large, shallow, food-rich lakes adjacent to it. Dewey's Pasture Wildlife Management Area and National Historic Landmark near Ruthven, Iowa. Photo by Tom Rothe.

CHAPTER 3
Substrate and Vegetation Structure

Marshes, like all plant communities, have certain physical or structural features (*life form* or *physiognomy*) that provide identifying characteristics.[18] In addition to water, the main visual clues are the tall *emergent* plants that form the perimeter and sometimes the center of a marsh. These are taller and more robust than most prairie grasses, yet not as tall nor as woody as trees. As we examine the marsh structure from shore to center, other plants occur, as well as water and basin characteristics that mechanically influence how animals are attracted to and use the community.

Substrate

The composition of the basin—whether of undifferentiated rock, stones, rubble, gravel, sand, or fine soils—dramatically influences the available nutrients, the rate of pioneering of plants on that substrate, the survival of plants, and the durability of the bottom itself. The character of this bottom also determines the nature of habitats available for invertebrates, fish (especially for spawning), and the influence of wave action on rooted plants. These generalizations will gain significance in later discussions of other structural components of the system as habitats for animals.

Water Depth Influences on Plants

The distribution of plants of various life forms determines a major structural feature of a marsh. Water depth is perhaps the dominant physical factor influencing the kind of adaptations required of the plant if it is to establish, live, and reproduce on a site.[158, 171, 172] The "strategy" used by the plant is a product of evolutionary adaptations that include reproductive system (seed or vegetative propagation), leaf form, stem or stalk form, root structure, water tolerance, salt tolerance, and other physiological parameters.[183]

Without going into detail with such matters, since they have been treated in several texts,[183] I will provide a few examples. Cattail is a well-known plant genus that dominates the wetlands round the world. The complexities of physical, biological, and physiological responses to water are so varied that the resultant, localized forms have confounded the scientific classification of cattails, and specialists disagree on whether some forms are hybrids or valid species. But more important for animal residents, cattails of various species, populations, or "stocks" grow in waters of various depths, creating food supplies for herbivorous insects and muskrats, structural support for bird nests or bird roosting, and structural material for nests of birds and semiaquatic mammals.[73, 124, 222]

But cattails aren't found everywhere; they have physiological and physical limits—as do all organisms. Field observation and greenhouse experiments show that some forms of cattail germinate and grow better in deep water, that they produce more underwater tubers (growth shoots) per plant, and that plant density (plants per unit area) is greater at optimal than maximal water depths.[222] The typical pattern in the Midwest is that broad-leaf cattail is found in shallow water at marsh edges or in more shallow, temporary wetland types, whereas narrow-leaf cattail tends to be in deeper water. A hybrid between these two is the most water tolerant of all, sometimes growing in three feet of water alongside hardstem bulrush. This hybrid is often the most common form found in large marshes. But at greater depths (over three feet), all species reach their physiological limits. Moreover, the physical influences of wave action, "rooting" muskrats, and fish (especially carp) cause flotation of the buoyant rootstocks,[226, 230] and the edge between a cattail bed and open water becomes a tension zone: The plant edge-water interface shifts back and forth from season to season with changes in water depth, wind action, and animal density.

At the shoreward edge of the wetland, it is probably the availability and constancy of moisture, competition with better-adapted shallow-

Islands of cattail in an impounded area of the Roseau River Wildlife Management Area, Minnesota. These islands are ideal areas for nesting ducks and coots. Dense beds of the submergent water milfoil are visible at the surface.

marsh plants, and perhaps nutrient dynamics that influence the success of cattail and hence their extent in the uplands edge.

The arrowhead, a species of wet meadow zones that are seasonally inundated, furnishes another example of the influence of water depth on plants. If, during drought, they become established in the marsh center and later are flooded, rather than arrow-shaped leaves, they develop linear (filiform) leaves that challenge experts to distinguish these from other normally underwater plants like wild celery. Often, as they reach the surface, their leaves broaden, the stems become more rigid, and they flower. Ultimately, at high water levels, they die out.

These examples demonstrate that plants found in a wetland are adaptable but also have limits, and that the life-history strategies of individual species collectively influence the kind of *community* of plants present. These, in turn, dictate what animals are present.

Plant Life-Forms

As a product of years of evolutionary adaptation, various groups of plants have evolved different strategies for different water depths,

Floating cattail disrupted by flooding of buoyant rootstocks, and possibly muskrat "rooting." Hardstem bulrush is in deeper water behind.

and they can be classified into several major groups: *Emergents* are plants that grow with their roots and often bases in wet soil or water part or all of their life. Examples, given from shallow to deeper water, are rice cutgrass, whitetop, sedges, softstem bulrush, river bulrush and other "threesquares," cattail, and hardstem bulrush. *Floating-leaf* plants are those rooted in deeper water that tend to send up broad, floating leaves to the surface where photosynthesis takes place. Nutrients move between leaves and massive tubers via flexible and slender stems that may be five or six feet long. Thus, such plants can grow in much deeper water than can most emergents, filling in otherwise open pools, and they survive well with fluctuating water levels. An example is yellow water lily. *Submergent* plants generally are rooted but have their stems and leaves mostly if not entirely underwater.[205] Characterized by fine, complex, and compound leaves growing in clusters, they seem to be efficient at gathering the vital light in even murky water. One group, bladderwort, has combined green leaves with tiny animal traps in which the plants catch

Submergent bladderwort, widespread throughout temperate and subtropical North America, has small animal traps that supplement its nutrient intake. The small floating plants are lesser duckweed, and the starlike plants near or under the surface are star duckweed.

and utilize minute crustaceans and protozoans. Numerous species flower at the water's surface and bring color to the marsh; yellow for bladderwort; white or yellow for water-crowfoot. Some like sago pondweed, form seed heads there—often excellent foods for insects and ducks. Other examples of submergents are water milfoil, and wigeongrass in alkaline or saline waters. *Floating* plants are not rooted and usually remain on the surface of the water. They seem to be fairly small in the northern latitudes, where, due to freeze-up, they are annuals; and they are larger in warmer climates, where they may be less influenced by seasonality. They are flowering plants with dangling roots that derive nutrients from the water. Such free-floating plants are strongly influenced in distribution by the wind, tending either to wind-row or to remain between protecting emergents, except in tiny wetlands where wind is less influential. Examples are lesser and greater duckweed and the introduced water hyacinth. Some floating plants, such as star duckweed, are found below the surface at various depths and drift with minute water movements induced by animal activity and probably differential heating.

The combination of life forms and species in a particular wetland constitute the living, dynamic, interactive plant community. Sometimes such plant communities last for several years; but most often they change from season to season. The question of why each plant exists in a certain marsh is outside the scope of this book, but some influences will be discussed later under marsh habitat dynamics. Our immediate concern is how these forms in themselves survive and influence other organisms in the community.

Marsh Islands, Edge, and Layers

Because marshes are formed in basins, they naturally are surrounded by uplands with diverse kinds of vegetation. These wetlands are thus habitats nearly as different as islands in a lake; indeed, there are some advantages in viewing these as "islands," since concepts of island biology have been fruitful approaches to understanding how animals and plants reach isolated habitats and are affected by the size, placement, and character of these habitat units.[224] Marsh basins become concentration areas of nutrient material in the form of decaying organic matter and minerals that wash in. The net productivity is high, and we can expect dense concentrations of living organisms that use the nutrients, and others that feed on those organisms. Concentrations of birds generally attract predators, but terrestrial predators are inhibited by the presence of water. Only a few specialized predators (mink, otter, and perhaps raccoon) regularly swim and live in or near water, even rearing their young there. Central marsh vegetation often is protected by water, and bird species not only concentrate there but tolerate a short near-neighbor distance, forming dense colonies—such as blackbirds, egrets, herons, and ibises— and realize a high reproductive success in the absence of predators. The same phenomenon occurs on small islands in lakes where gulls, terns, and ducks have higher-than-average egg success in a predator-free environment, and they and their offspring return to breed regularly.[111, 215]

Rock or soil islands or islands of bulrushes, reeds or trees in marshes, and even muskrat lodges, have an especially dramatic effect on species richness of birds and how birds place nests or obtain food. Islands, like irregularly shaped marshes, create additional edge, and some evidence exists that marsh-upland edges or cover-water edges increase population density of some bird species and bird species richness.[18]

In the same way, the lack of emergent vegetation in a marsh causes an opening, or pool, often in the center but possible anywhere in slightly deeper water. The size, abundance, and distribution of such pools modify the amount of cover-water edge and the access to cover, and seem to be important in creating more diverse habitats for birds.

The marsh edge-water interface is equally important for the more aquatic species such as fish. Even fish that live in open water may spawn and grow in the protection and shallows of marshy areas. More aquatic birds such as pied-billed grebes and diving ducks may feed on animals and plants in open ponds or lake, but nest and rear their young in the emergent plants of marshes or marsh edge.

Another recent approach to understanding habitat influences on animal distribution is the concept of specialization of some animals for particular habitats. In forests, layers of strata of vegetation are important influences on the numbers or species present, since some birds are adapted to tree tops, some to trunks, and some to understory vegetation or ground cover. Generally speaking, the more strata, the more places for different species to feed or nest. Marsh-nesting birds also use several different layers: water level (such as pied-billed grebes); low vegetation near water level (coots, several ducks, rails); robust emergents like cattail (blackbirds, egrets); and marsh edge trees (orioles, wood ducks).[226]

CHAPTER 4
The Marsh as a System

Because all organisms require food for their survival, growth, and reproduction, much of the behavioral and physiological activities of plants and animals is devoted to food-getting. A study of a marsh community focusing on the food interrelationships of its members will reveal much about the efficiency and the total energy of the system.

Various organisms in the wetland community play different *roles*, and the system can function well only when all components are present and effective. Plants fill the role of *primary producer*, converting water and carbon dioxide into carbohydrates through the energy of sunlight and the action of chlorophyll. A few marsh and bog plants are *carnivorous*, but their greenery suggests that trapped animals fill only part of their food requirement. But plants also create a physical environment, trapping heat, reducing wind, stabilizing soil, and providing substrates as well as food for animals. All animals are dependent on plant producers; thus, we can't discuss animals alone in any ecological sense. Those animals using only plant food directly are termed *herbivores*, and are the *primary consumers* in the flow of energy through the system (measured as calories). Some animals feed on the herbivores and are, therefore carnivores, in a secondary consumer role; those higher carnivores that feed on secondary consumers may be termed tertiary consumers. Some animals, *omnivores*, use both plants and animals as food. An often unappreciated group of organisms (the *detritivores*) assist in the decomposition of organic material resulting from growth of plants such as emergents. Some of these are *shredders* like muskrats that eat some small portion of the total emergent plant production but shred still more in cutting for lodges and selecting food, thereby creating smaller pieces. In stream systems, there may be five or six insect or other invertebrate groups that cut and shred various sizes of plant debris until it can be used by smaller and smaller organisms. Physical action like water and wind also helps to produce detritus from larger plants or animals. Eventually, microscopic *decomposer* organisms like bacteria and fungi may act on the organic matter, further decomposing it and creating organic wastes usable by still other tiny organisms. Ultimately, nitrogen and phosphorus, vital to protein synthesis and energy metabolism, respectively, and other important elements must be available. Without this return of nutrients to the system, productivity declines and the whole ecological system suffers.

Food Chains and Webs

Specialization for foods in a marsh habitat is no different from that in other communities, except that animals adapted to marshes have to be able to move in and around water and take food from water as well as near it. Terrestrial herbivores readapted to the marsh by virtue of webbed feet (birds and mammals), heavier down (birds), or water tolerant fur (mammals) would not be likely to change their food habits greatly. Thus, the muskrat is a member of the subfamily of field mice (Microtinae), but it has webbed feet and a flattened tail useful in swimming, and water-resistant fur groomed regularly to insure dryness and warmth.[60] But it is merely a well-adapted plant feeder that utilizes marsh emergents (cattail, bulrush, arrowhead) rather than terrestrial grasses. It builds a nest of shredded vegetation like other field mice but may locate it inside a massive lodge of cut marsh plants, usually built in the fall before winter freeze-up.[59] This herbivore plays the same role as a herbivorous insect. This is an example of the most simple and direct of all *food chains*, moving energy from the plant that produces the food to the tissue of the primary consumer, with some loss in tissue conversion and in metabolism by a mobile organism.[29, 153] Among truly aquatic forms, the consumption of algae by small free-swimming *zooplankton* (protozoans and crustaceans) which in turn are eaten by small minnows, which subsequently may be eaten by larger fish, provides a classic

Muskrat feeding on cattail alongside its lodge. Lodges may contain nests and families, or groups of five to eight individuals of various ages.

example of a longer food chain involving secondary and tertiary consumers.

Most food chains are not tightly structured because animals must be opportunistic feeders, using what is available at a given time. As a result, food interrelationships are so complex they are spoken of as a *food web*. In certain situations, animals that are normally prey may become predators. Omnivores have especially great flexibility, which may explain why this group is so numerous. Muskrats, normally herbivorous, may feed opportunistically on clams (whether by nutrient deficiency, local habit, or design); blackbirds may feed their young on invertebrates from the marsh or fly some distance to gather terrestrial insects where they can. Herons, which normally feed on fish and amphibians, may eat other birds' eggs, terrestrial snakes or small mammals, and diverse other foods. Their basic foraging behavior and predatory habits are generally unchanged, regardless of their foods, but they adapt to food availability readily. Little blue herons often follow mergansers and pied-billed grebes that are feeding on fish, the herons apparently catching some fish attempting to escape from the underwater divers.[55] This effective adaptation is accomplished by "association" rather than "calculation," but it works!

These organisms are part of the complex system of nutrient movement through the community, so obviously the supply of various nutrients controls the relative "richness" of the system.

Nutrients

Basins may be relatively infertile when they are new, containing few nutrients or an inadequate balance of nutrients. Inflowing water enriched in phosphorus, nitrogen, potassium, calcium, and other nutrients adds to those nutrients present to create a more productive system.[100] Nutrient enrichment also takes place by wind-blown or water-moved soil, as has been shown in prairie wetlands.[1] Moreover, the vegetative cover on the surrounding uplands strongly influences the erosion of soil into the wetland as well as the nutrient buildup. Increased organic matter also may enter the system in the form of detritus or by way of the invasion of live plants from the shallow to deeper areas.

Water areas are classified by nutrient content and productivity; most marshes are rich or *eutrophic* because of the organic buildup; lakes are often more sterile, or *oligotrophic*.[153] Such nutrient levels are reflected in the richness of plants, invertebrates, and even water birds.[167, 212, 221] Where cold temperatures slow the chemical processes in plants themselves, production is naturally low at all levels, and evolution of the system is slower. Therefore, time, temperature, seasonality of growing seasons, and other environmental factors influence the buildup of nutrients. In some Antarctic ponds, it seems certain that excrements from birds and seals—the foods of which come from the sea—are the major source of nutrients for unicellular aquatic plants responsible for energy trapping and subsequent food chains. Concentrations of birds in wetlands also may alter water quality and characteristics,[71, 87, 132] and farm drainages from livestock holding areas may quickly enrich wetlands and modify the nature of the vegetation there.

Experimental studies of nutrients in marshes have shown that the marsh system is strongly influenced by the nature of the incoming water (including pollutants), and that the marsh modifies all chemical parameters of water as water flows through the system.[102] Particulate matter such as soil and organic debris tends to be deposited in the marsh basin. Heavy metals are immobilized and often deposited. Some dissolved constituents are trapped and held in the marsh (*uptake* and *storage*), most *cycle* through the components of the system, and some are lost.

Limited studies of primary production and nutrient cycling in the marsh system have provided a basis for some general concepts of the steps in the energy flow through a marsh system. Because of the typical anaerobic conditions at the bottom of a marsh, decomposition and mineralization of organic materials is slower than in terrestrial systems. The general scheme seems to be that the emergent aquatic plants that characterize marshes are the ones that tap the above-water-level oxygen and the nutrient pool stored in the soil substrate and build major organic structures.[214] Submergent plants, which also are rooted and obtain nutrients from the substrate, must constitute a major proportion of the nutrient flow in shallow open marshes or lakes.[31] Such plants—emergent and submergent—are referred to as *nutrient pumps* because they move phosphorus from the substrate to the plant and eventually, by decomposition, to the water. The major weight of biological organisms in the marsh ecosystem usually is represented by the larger emergent plants. In marshes, this net primary productivity is enormous, exceeding that of grasslands and equaling or exceeding that of many forests. For example, the metric tons of emergent plant per hectare per growth season has been estimated as follows: sedge = 10; reed = 21; and cattail = 27. Such emergents constitute the dominant plant structure as well as the greatest production unit in the marsh. Phytoplankton and free-floating plants take nutrients directly from the water and may constitute especially large biomass in open, lake-like marshes.

Nutrient movement through the marsh takes place through decomposition and/or herbivore utilization of these major energy concentrations; herbivores break down the plant biomass and speed the process. Some nutrients are leached from the plants by water, and other plant materials become detritus that is devoured by secondary consumers, ultimately to return to the category of available nutrients.[48] The key nutrients for plant growth, nitrogen and phosphorus, are easily tied up in the sediments or the biomass, which action seems to limit plant growth and hence production of the entire system.

Excessive enrichment occurs especially when phosphorus is added to a lake experimentally or accidentally, and eutrophication results.[178] Algae and floating plants that take nutrients directly from the water tend to dominate and may shade out other plants as well as reduce available oxygen for animals. Microscopic and filamentous algae, floating duckweeds, and watermeal dominate such systems.

CHAPTER 5
Some Aspects
of Marsh Communities

Although we will later review some of the major animals of marshes by taxonomic categories (insects, birds, etc.), it is important to recognize that the individual species of marsh communities often have evolved together and may form a distinctive and functional entity. Some of the characteristics of the components of the eco-system were mentioned earlier, but before examining the marsh fauna, we should consider several additional ideas. In most cases, I will use examples of birds, because these are the ones I know best.

Animal Adaptations

It is generally assumed that early life had its origin in water and that many species and groups are still restricted to that environment. Fish and many invertebrates such as clams and crustaceans live underwater, obtaining their oxygen and food there. But organisms adapted to shallow water had to evolve adaptive mechanisms for survival in times of drought, or the drying of a pond might totally eliminate a population or even a species. Thus, drought-resistant eggs, which respond quickly to reflooding, and short life cycles are characteristic of many species of microscopic protozoans, crustaceans, and insects (especially mosquitoes). Those insects like dragonflies that have immature stages lasting several years are characteristic of more permanent water.[106]

But clearly many of the abundant and conspicuous vertebrate

forms like birds and mammals did not evolve in water but are re-adapted to the aquatic system, probably because of its rich resources. Obviously, habitat adaptation requires major anatomic modifications for surface locomotion (swimming, wading) or for specialized flight within a restricted environment (hovering and diving by terns; vertical takeoff by ducks using small wetlands). And even marsh perching presents special difficulties. Imagine the typical sparrow trying to hang onto the slippery, vertical stalks of marsh reeds. Wrens and yellow-headed blackbirds do it neatly, using a "spread-eagle" technique with one foot on each of two stalks. For these reasons, fewer semiaquatic vertebrates than invertebrates are well adapted, and some have adaptive strategies, only using wetlands when convenient. Many simply must avoid the rich resources of this habitat because their specializations are for terrestrial habitats, such as grassland, shrubs, and trees.

Competition and Resource Segregation

A long-held concept of ecology has been that no two species may occupy the same niche and exploit the same resources.[153] But much ecological research today is directed toward the ways in which species do seem to accomplish this. Competition for resources brings about specializations that reduce direct conflict. The presence of competitors narrows habitat selection, and the variety of species in a community seems to depend on their ability to survive without excessive competition. Many diverse mechanisms have evolved: feeding at different times of day or night, variations in seasonal use of foods or areas, different foods, similar foods in different habitats, size of foods, and so on. The result is that a marsh can have a large number of bird species, mostly secondary or tertiary consumers, which seem to make use of extremely abundant resources without severe competition, and some of which feed on different resources in different places in sometimes different ways, so that competition does not limit their presence. The waterfowl (ducks, geese, and swans) are a good example: Swans and wigeon feed on submergent plants in water, or on fine grasses along seasonally flooded shorelines. Geese feed on drier sites on sedges and grasses, and some feed on the tubers (for example, snow geese) whereas others feed on stems and leaves (Canada geese). Many dabbling ducks are omnivores, consuming seeds and foliage at some times of the year[26] (usually winter) and feeding on more invertebrates in the prebreeding period (especially the females, which need special nutrients for egg laying).[112, 113] The apparent use of similar resources by dabbling ducks such as mallards and blue-winged teal in similar feeding sites has not been adequately explained, but often the sites have superabundant food resources. Inland diving ducks feed on bottom organisms like snails, clams, and midge larvae in water depths that require diving. Sea ducks use different habitats and are almost purely animal feeders, taking some very large, hard objects, such as mollusks (eiders), or fast-swimming but large prey like fish (mergansers). Thus, the various groups are well segregated by their habitat selection as well as by their food, and many seem to feed side by side with little of the aggressiveness seen among potential competitors. We shall examine some other examples of *resource segregation* as we later review some of the dominant groups of animals characteristic of a midwestern marsh.

Social Relationships

Interspecific social relationships are strongly influenced by the increased concentration of a species' population in the marsh. Some birds are dense colony nesters; some nest in a loose colony; others remain solitary, but may cluster because of the patchiness of suitable habitat. Egrets and ibises, eared grebes, and yellow-headed blackbirds are typical colony nesters. Nests of western grebes and some ducks may be found in clusters in suitable habitats.

Breeding behavior patterns are closely tied to the clustering of nest sites, and although monogamy is still the common practice of marsh birds, the predictably abundant food resources permits multiple mating systems (polygamy).[154] The males of several species of marsh blackbirds and of both long-billed and sedge wrens seem to mate with as many females as they can accommodate in their territory. Possibly because the females can find an adequate amount of food for feeding the young, males can devote their efforts to territorial defense. But even within a productive marsh, sites do vary in quality (although we have difficulty quantifying what attracts a nesting female to a particular site), and some male redwings will establish territories in places where few or no females will nest. Other males end up with four or five females.

The social system of a particular species may benefit several different species in the marsh community. For example, blackbirds, terns, and gulls are constantly alert to potential predators such as hawks, mink, or man; each has a special alarm call, and most engage in mobbing behavior. Such behavior not only alerts individuals of the same species, but seems to alarm other species as well (as any hunter or birder can attest!). An incubating duck on the nest becomes alert as a tern calls overhead, and hens with ducklings are even more wary. These interspecific warning signals clearly function for the good of all in the community.

Sounds of the Marsh

Birds and amphibians as well as insects create the sounds that we know as a marsh: One can be in a plowed field or a dense forest and know a marsh is just over the hill. Marsh sounds are not always pleasing, for bird calls can be harsh, and insects buzz or drone. Some typical sounds of the community can carry over the noise of water and wind in reeds.

Dominant in these vocalizations at night are the leopard frogs and American toad. The mating calls of males attract females, and the marsh may be simply swarming with toads or frogs at certain seasons and in some years.

Different insects may be active at different times of night or day, and most produce buzzing sounds, such as those of mosquitoes or midges. Hordes of midges make an impressive drone, and those who believe them to be biting insects would be understandably concerned. Fortunately, they are merely a nuisance during peak swarms, when they may coat everything, including human eyes, ears, nose, and mouth.

But it is the bird sounds for which a marsh is best known. In the Midwest, these include the raucous "poppycock" call of the male yellow-headed blackbird, the "creee-e-e" of the redwinged blackbird, the resounding "thunderpumping" of the American bittern, the winnowing series of chirps of rails, the sharp alarm calls of terns overhead, the "churking" of coots, and the various hornlike or laughter-like calls of several species of grebes.

Marshes bring diversity in many ways, their sounds among the most fascinating; though sometimes harsh, they reflect the richness of the marsh.

The Marsh Edge

The transition zone between two plant communities may form a broad ecotone, as in the case of the prairie and deciduous forest in the Midwest, or it may be abrupt, forming a discrete edge. Either type of edge strongly influences animal distribution, as noted among birds; but the interface between marsh edge and upland is notable for other reasons. First, it is a dynamic front, where many species of plants characteristic of moist soil or periodically flooded zones are found. The plants may be shorter, and richer in species, than either the marsh itself or the upland zones. There may be distinct zones of vegetation that germinated during certain water levels, or the plant community may be mixed. Such moist soil zones are made up of plants characteristic of any very shallow and temporarily flooded wetland, or drawdown conditions in an emergent marsh that induce moist-soil vegetation over extensive bare areas. Animals too may be diverse in this zone, depending on the mix of plants and the water level. Quite open mudflat areas may be frequented by killdeer or other shorebirds and waders. Frogs of several species use wet meadows adjacent to marshes. Black-birds do likewise, and bitterns and herons may catch meadow mice as well as insects in such areas. Some bird species like swamp sparrows and yel-lowthroats are in their prime habitat here; this is where they nest, although they may stray some distance into the uplands or into the marsh to forage. Some terrestrial blackbirds fly hundreds of yards from the marsh to seek insect foods for their nestlings, although adult males and nonbreeders may feed on waste agricultural grains as well. Some species, like the mallard and blue-winged teal, nest in the uplands or at the marsh edge but feed in the marsh during the breeding period. They are plagued by such terrestrial predators as skunks, raccoons, and ground squirrels, but their persistent nesting behavior helps to compensate for high losses.

Mink and raccoons concentrate along the marsh edge, where they can move in the not-so-dense cover and capture crayfish, mice, and frogs. Deer have well-defined trails leading to the marsh, where they drink, and they find shelter in the willow thickets, reed, or cattail beds, but they prefer the drier sites for bedding down. Thus, a strong evolutionary influence of the upland-marsh interface exists because marshes often go dry; those adapted to the edge are always present, whereas aquatic specialists must leave, or die.

But the most vital aspect of this interface may be biochemical, for here the marsh gains additional nutrients from rainfall, drainage, and seepage through upland soils. Nutrients from decaying plants and animals eventually find their way downward to the marsh basin. Masses of swallows that feed in the marsh and roost at the edge by day and in the marsh at night "whitewash" large areas, eventually adding many nutrients to the marsh ecosystem.

CHAPTER 6
Dominant Animals

A brief review of the dominant animals, concentrating on the more conspicuous wildlife of midwestern marshes, will document the impressive variety found in even a small area, the unseen as well as the seen. Their use of this unique system dramatizes habitat selection and segregation among closely related species, showing the roles these forms play in the functioning of the ecosystem. We will consider these by taxonomic groups, but without neglecting habitat selection, roles, relationships, and species associations. We'll start with the most conspicuous, the birds, and end with the most inconspicuous but perhaps most important in the system, the invertebrates.

Birds

Although generalizations are inherently dangerous in their lack of flexibility, a description of some general patterns may help the reader to place species in perspective with others and to appreciate the evolutionary forces that have induced habitat use, breeding behavior, and use of space by birds. The marsh has been a strong attraction to bird groups not only because of its food richness but also because it provides nesting, resting, and feeding sites protected from ground predators. Various groups have adapted anatomically to such aquatic situations to the extreme that they are less efficient on land (loons, grebes, and inland diving ducks); others use upland as well as aquatic habitats and have added flexibility, but certain disadvantages too (dabbling ducks, some waders, rails); numerous species use the marsh edge as the focal point of their feeding and breeding (swamp sparrows, sedge wrens, and redwinged blackbirds). Actually, some whole orders (the major taxonomic divisions within the class of birds) have specialized in aquatic habitats, and various subgroups (families, genera, species) have adapted in varying degrees. We will discuss variation in closely related species (Fig. 2), considering generally how they use different habitats and foods.[226] Most breeding birds are carnivores or omnivores, and only rarely herbivores in the marsh. As we shall see, use of marshes, habitats, and foods varies seasonally as influenced by needs for reproduction or by availability in the system. Well-adapted aquatic species are limited to marshes or lakes year-round even if they migrate long distances, and they use few if any terrestrial foods (inland diving ducks, for example). Marsh-edge species also tend to seek out similar habitats all year, but they have greater flexibility, seeking food in uplands as well as in marsh areas (geese).

It is impossible to consider all the birds in a typical marsh, but a few examples of dominant groups will demonstrate the pattern: Loons (or divers) normally use the deeper, more sterile water of large lakes, but common loons may use marshes in northern Minnesota and Wisconsin where deep water holds a fish population. Grebes of

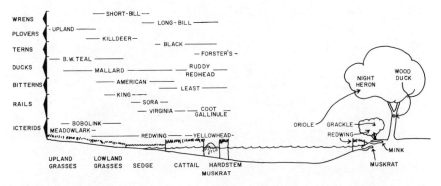

Figure 2. *Competition for nest sites and associated food commonly brings about the segregation of closely related species into adjacent habitats with reduced overlap. Whole families of birds may be tied to wetlands, such as herons and bitterns or rails, whereas other families of birds (icterids) have numerous upland representatives as well as those adapted to the marsh.[226] Thus, in a given region of a marsh (open water edge), or in a marsh that is entirely of that type (deep marsh), one can predict the species to be found there by their habitat preference.*

several species prefer marshy areas, especially during the nesting season, but all may feed along the seashore in winter. Grebes are so specialized with their rear-mounted legs that they walk poorly on land. The largest North American species, the western grebe, uses open areas and nests in extensive beds of reeds and other emergents. Red-necked grebes, horned grebes, and eared grebes use different types of wetlands according to preferences for pond size and density of cover.[64] Eared grebes are especially colonial but are restricted in distribution by their need for suitable habitat. The solitary pied-billed grebe is the most widespread, tolerating quite dense to quite open situations, and is very responsive to new habitats, perhaps because it is versatile in food selection, using invertebrates, fish, and amphibians taken mostly underwater.[163, 226] Although all grebes build low, wet nests made of submergent or emergent plants, the pied-bill is best known for its nest, usually a floating mass of rotting vegetation that is inconspicuous; its egg success is quite high.[184]

The ducks range from upland nesters that use water for dabble feeding,[51] loafing, and brood-rearing (blue-winged teal) to diving

The rotting cattail stems of which this Pied-bill Grebe nest was built probably warm as well as humidify the eggs.

forms like ruddy ducks that rarely leave the water. Ruddy ducks walk poorly on land, nest over water, and obtain foods almost entirely by diving. Most ducks are omnivores, but during laying, the females use a pure invertebrate diet essential for egg production. One duck that specializes on animal foods year-round is the shoveler. With its spatulate bill and fine lateral lamellae (strainers), the shoveler is the whale of the duck world, straining out fine plankton that less specialized bills could not efficiently utilize. It is not so specialized that it cannot consume seeds and larger invertebrates, however. One duck, the wigeon, specializes on leafy plant foods, and feeds on various succulent submergent and emergent plants. Its bill is shorter than that of most dabbling ducks and more gooselike. The canvasback has a long, sloping bill and dives for tubers of sago pondweed.

But the geese and swans are the major marsh herbivores, and it is not surprising that they are the larger-bodied birds, with long necks for reaching remote foods (the cattle of the waterfowl world). No specialized divers occur among geese and swans (although fulvous whistling ducks, which are closely related to the swans, dive well), but considerable variation exists in habitat choice, from dry-land geese that take their young to pond edges to feed and into the water for safety, to swans that nest over water and feed mostly on submerged aquatics.

Of the heronlike birds, the bitterns are perhaps the most closely associated with water. The most aquatic bittern is the least bittern, which builds a delicate, solitary nest several feet above water in cattail or bulrush, and feeds on frogs and other marsh animals of suitable size. It is rarely observed from shore and, unless one knows its dovelike call, it can be present in abundance and never recorded by "birders" who choose not to get their feet wet. The big American bittern is found mostly along the marsh edge, where it feeds on mammals and snakes as well as frogs, but it may penetrate the cattail or reed zone to build a solitary nest over water. However, upland nesting by bitterns is common in some drier prairie areas.

Herons, egrets, and ibises generally nest colonially in wetlands, also feeding there. Herons and most egrets feed on fish, frogs, and invertebrates in shallow marshy areas, and the black-crowned night heron occasionally even swims to catch fish. But there are exceptions: Ibises and storks nest in water-protected sites of deep marshes but feed in the wet meadows and uplands on animals. The pioneering cattle egret that reached the United States from South America in the early 1950s feeds in the uplands, where it catches arthropods disturbed by grazers. Depending on the time and place, great blue herons may nest in emergent vegetation or in trees in upland settings, but the best protected nests I've seen were in sprawling beds of prickly pear cactus on spoil islands along the intracoastal waterway in Texas. Clearly, marsh birds are flexible, and localized behavior patterns are common.

Terns are the insect gleaners and shallow fishermen of the marsh system.[21] Black terns feed mostly on insects at the water's surface, whereas Forster's terns feed on small fish in larger pools. Black terns nest only on low, soggy debris of old muskrat lodges, or build similar low nests of wet (old or new) vegetation.[45] Forster's terns may build larger and drier nests than do black terns, but they most often nest on high, dry muskrat lodges.[150] Forster's terns seem to get along with muskrats fairly well, as their nests are rarely lost to muskrat activity, possibly because muskrats do little lodge building at this season of the year.[226] Both tern species may have grouped nests when conditions are good, but rarely are they found in huge colonies, as are common in other gulls[4] and terns.

The rail family has representatives that span all the habitats of a typical marsh. The most aquatic representatives are the American coot and the common gallinule, which nest over water and feed their young on aquatic invertebrates. Coots are excellent divers and older young and adults feed on submergent vegetation, whereas gallinules are more surface-pickers and tend to occur in or close to heavily vegetated areas. Virginia rails and soras often are present in large marshes and often are heard, but not seen, because of their preference for dense vegetation. Virginia rails tend to use wetter sites in more robust vegetation, often nesting in shallow stands of cattail. Soras favor sedges in shallow water, but they also can be found well out in wet areas. The largest rail, the king rail, generally nests and feeds in marsh edges or upland areas and has, therefore, suffered more severe losses of habitat.

Blackbirds are conspicuous and abundant residents of marshes, with some species essentially restricted in nesting to flooded marsh emergents. In the Midwest, the yellow-headed blackbird is the central marsh resident, and the redwinged blackbird reaches its peak density along the edge.[226] During the breeding season, young are fed almost purely on invertebrates, but adults regularly feed on grain and other seeds as well as insects.[155, 216] Redwings are a highly social species, and often are polygynous; males in especially favored habitats may have two to five nesting females, sometimes successively.

Two wrens are common in, and nearly restricted to, marshes over a wide geographic area. Again, they overlap little. The long-billed marsh wren nests over water in robust vegetation such as cattail or hard-stemmed bulrush, whereas the sedge wren favors tall wet meadow grasses and even wet prairie vegetation. Both are insect feeders, gleaning the vegetation more than feeding in water. Polygyny also is common, with large numbers of dummy nests being built by the agile, vocal, and hyperactive male.

Several other passerines favor marsh edges, such as the swamp sparrow and yellowthroat. Swamp sparrows forage in the marsh edge but may use taller vegetation in damp sites for song perches and nest sites. Yellowthroats may nest in much drier upland sites as well, but seem to prefer wet areas.

Obviously, birds are an adaptable group. Any plant life form has its characteristic cluster of bird species, with little overlap of closely related species—and seemingly little competition for food, cover, or other resources (see Fig. 2). However, if for some reason one species is missing in an area, such as occurs in the timing of migration of redwing and yellow-headed blackbirds, the first to arrive (redwings) take over much of the marsh but later may be displaced by the more dominant yellow-heads. Hence, there is still some latitude in habitat use by many species, and more research is needed to fully measure and assess these complex interactions.

Also obvious is that most breeding marsh birds are carnivores, and probably have adapted to the marsh because of this rich resource of invertebrates. There are few plant feeders in early summer, but in late summer and fall, when seeds are most abundant, many young birds switch to seeds or leafy vegetation and exploit the seasons' greatest production. Birds en route to and on wintering areas often take more vegetable material in their diets.

Mammals

Relatively few mammals are truly marsh specialists. This is a seemingly major adaptation, one that cannot be complete; the effects could be disastrous for a nonmigratory population, because of the seasonal and annual fluctuations in water levels and marsh quality. Beavers compensate for fluctuating water levels by damming streams and creating their own stable pond. Otters adapt through maintenance of strong terrestrial behavior and through their flexibility in using streams, lakes, or ponds; but they seem to find marshes too short of large fish to spend much time there. However, otters are very abundant in coastal fresh and salt marshes of the Gulf Coast, where they feed on crayfish, crabs, and mammals as well as fish.[37a]

The lesser numbers of species of mammals is more than compensated for by the relative importance of these few specialists in the functioning of the system. The widespread muskrat and the nutria (introduced from South America) constitute the major herbivorous, mammalian specialists. Interestingly, these animals probably evolved in two of the most extensive marsh-dominated areas of the world, the Prairie Pothole Region of the United States and the Pampas marshes of Argentina. But both herbivores are fairly adaptable and are found in a variety of aquatic and wetland habitats. All use a great variety of vegetation as food but all grazers favor growing shoots, because of their concentrated nutrients, or rootstocks and tubers, which store nutrients for subsequent growing seasons. Muskrats and their close relatives, the round-tailed muskrat or water rat of Florida, and the nutria build nest "balls" for rearing their young; these balls are made of shredded vegetation and are lodged in sturdy vegetation above the water level. Beavers also get into large and fairly stable marshes,[17] either because of regional preference or as stream populations overflow. In such situations, beavers may build lodges of and eat cattail instead of willows or cottonwood, but I know of no studies of their survival or reproductive success in such situations.

All three herbivores, but especially muskrats and beaver, influence marshes more by their cutting of vegetation for lodges, storage, and nests than by their cutting for food consumption. In the north, these lodges provide protection against the cold and heavy snow, as well as a food supply that may be exploited in late winter or early spring, when resources are at their seasonal low. Muskrat lodges are built quickly in the late summer and early fall, when the vegetation has reached its peak. Some are 6 feet high and 15 feet in diameter, and terrestrial plants may grow on them. They may be abandoned after one season and settle into the water from autumn rain and winter

The muskrat lodge, a product of the marsh and of a marsh specialist, the muskrat, is in itself a fascinating "island" utilized by many forms of life. In addition to terns and ducks that may nest upon it, muskrats, mice, raccoon, or mink that may lodge within it, there are mites and insects that live in the plant stalks, eating, decomposing, preying on, being preyed on, and so on. "Scuds" and snails below the water level devour rotting vegetation, and minnows and bullheads find food and shelter in the passageways.

snow; they are enriched by bird and muskrat droppings; and they may become germination sites of semiaquatic plants. The pools formed where lodges were built remain open for a long time in some situations, resistant to plant growth for reasons still not clear; these open pools are favored by birds for several years.

More species of carnivores use marshes, but they are less specialized. The otter is more truly aquatic, frequenting deeper water, where it utilizes fish as a major food. The mink is a more typical marsh associate—often tied to muskrat populations—although mink inhabit streams and lakes as well. But especially during the breeding season, the easiest place to find mink is along the edge of a marsh. Trails along the shoreline of wet meadow are conspicuous, and remains of prey and tell-tale droppings denote catches and feeding sites. In an old muskrat burrow at the base of a near-flooded willow tree, or in a muskrat lodge itself, piles of droppings, feathers, wings, and mammal fur tell of a litter of young. Muskrats are perhaps the major food of mink in these situations but crayfish, frogs, fish, and small mammals also are taken.

Several other mustelids frequent marshes, with short-tailed weasels being reasonably common in the North Central region. Least weasels, the smallest of the group, have one of the most northerly of ranges and even frequent Alaskan tundra areas. Such weasels probably favor mice and birds for food and may use old bird nest sites as resting areas.

Although raccoons often are found in terrestrial and even woodland habitat, some populations—at least in summer—use marsh edges and muskrat lodges. More than once I've encountered a raccoon curled up in a muskrat lodge far from shore. Trails along the marsh edge are usually littered with the remains of crayfish—a favorite of raccoons—and droppings suggesting that these remains are mainly prey items captured by raccoons.

Meadow mice and short-tailed shrews frequent marsh edges, and our small mammal trapping in northwest Iowa has demonstrated higher densities in wet meadows along marshes than in higher and drier bluegrass and prairie grasses. Meadow mice do swim, and occasionally even nest in muskrat lodges or the bases of duck nests. Whether this behavior is forced by water fluctuation or is a localized habitat selection trait is uncertain, but I know of no real measure of population densities of any marsh mammals other than muskrats and nutria.

These mammals are good examples of the food pyramid, wherein a few primary consumers efficiently convert large amounts of plant resources into plant debris, which is broken down by detritivores and is converted into animal protein. Muskrats are present in dense numbers, trappers sometimes taking 15 to 20 per acre. Mink, being higher in the food chain, are few in number and must expend great amounts of energy in the search for and capture of their prey. In addition to the mink fur's greater durability than muskrat fur (do mink work harder or is it the protective water environment?), the reduced supply increases demand and explains why mink coats cost more.

Fish

Relatively little is known about fish in marshes, but the marsh environment limits the kinds that can live and, especially, reproduce there. Because of the shallower depths, reduced wind action, higher water temperature, reduced oxygen, and sometimes more turbid water, larger fish are those we associate with highly eutrophic systems: bullheads and introduced carp. But water depths vary seasonally, and oxygen needs and tolerance vary with ages of the fish. The northern marsh canoeist is impressed in the spring when a streak underwater denotes the presence of northern pike that enter lakeshore marshes to breed. Later in the season, predation on ducklings is another measure of their presence.[119] But young pike move out of the marsh and spend most of their adult lives in more open water. For northern pike, this relationship of marsh to lake is so vital that fish populations decline when water levels prevent spawning and rearing in such areas.[67, 110] Other fish also come to spawn, and young (especially the preyed-upon) find protective cover in the emergent and submergent vegetation and may remain in these rearing areas until quite mature.[88, 162]

But the larger predatory fish probably are not as important in the energy flow in a marsh as they are in lakes, and the predatory niche often is filled by herons. Although factual data on fish populations are difficult to obtain in a marshy situation, it has been done with various drop-traps or scoop nets.[118a] Clearly much more work needs to be done with this group of vertebrates. I suspect that masses of tiny sticklebacks, various minnows, or other minnow-sized fishes are the major underwater primary (plant), secondary, or tertiary (animal) consumers in the marsh system. Certainly when larger predatory fish enter the marshes, even if briefly, they feed on these smaller fish readily. The importance of these fish to storks and herons is fully appreciated,[28] but this important food chain needs more intensive study.

Amphibians

Salamanders, frogs, and toads represent specializations from the most to the least aquatic amphibians that use marshes. But like fish, their niches and habitats differ with age.

Larval amphibians are aquatic and feed on minute plants and animals, but as adults, they gradually shift to animal food of larger sizes, including minnows and invertebrates. The adults may be totally predaceous, but their range in foods probably changes by habitat as well as by season. Salamanders are highly aquatic, but some species, like tiger salamanders, move overland in large numbers at times, though probably more because of the breeding seasons or wintering areas than because of food needs. These animals can be major food items for birds like white pelicans that use marshes and shallow lakes to gather food for their young.[125] Frogs, such as the common leopard frog, use both shallow aquatic areas and wet meadows, where we have often taken them in traps designed for small mammals.

The giant bullfrog of warmer southern and eastern waters is a significant predator on larger prey items, taking other frogs and even ducklings. Toads, of course, are more terrestrial, turning up in very dry sites long distances from water, but in the spring, it is the marsh where they chorus, mate, and breed. The eggs hatch and the young grow in the warm, food-rich, and protected shallow waters. As young, schools of tadpoles are conspicuous along marsh margins, seemingly so vulnerable that one wonders how they reach maturity. But the jab of a stick, like the jab of a heron, produces a coordinated predator-escape response that demonstrates how schooling benefits the majority. Amphibians are prime food sources for all the larger predators such as mink, raccoons, herons, bitterns, and fish.

Reptiles

Three major groups of reptiles occur in wetlands in various parts of the country. Of these, turtles are the most widespread geographically and the most common in number of species or population size. Species vary from place to place, but the sight of turtles basking in the sun is as common in marshes as it is in lakes—only the sunning site is more likely a muskrat lodge than a rock or log. Although painted and mud turtles are common, less often seen is the massive, predatory, snapping turtle that slips slowly and silently underneath its prey and helps to reduce overpopulation in a local area. Its prey is diverse, including fish, frogs, and birds.

Snakes are also fairly common in marshes, but perhaps less so than in swamps and river wetlands. In the northern marshes, the only regular resident is the garter snake, which seems mainly to patrol the marsh edge where it takes eggs and young from redwinged blackbird nests, but it does not fear water and occasionally is found basking on a muskrat lodge.

Southern marshes, usually the deeper ones, are dominated by the largest and most feared of all reptiles, the alligator. Each has its "hole" that seems to be dug out and retains water even in the drier periods. Their role as a major predator on birds and mammals must be significant, yet herons still wade, coots still swim, and water rats still nest adjacent to alligator "holes."

Invertebrates

Because these generally smaller animals are so diverse, representing thousands of species, I mention here only a few of the dominant, macroscopic groups that play significant roles in the marsh system.[106, 147, 161, 219] Several rare but unique groups occur such as the freshwater jellyfish and freshwater sponges, but it is the ubiquitous forms, regardless of size, that are principal food resources for the wide range of vertebrate predators already discussed. They are the core of the marsh food chains and webs. Many are predators themselves, like the dragonfly nymph that catches minnows or the adult dragonfly that catches mosquitoes on the wing. Tiny swimming protozoans and crustaceans are trapped by bladderwort plants, large crustaceans also catch all kinds of small crustaceans, insects, and so on, and a wide range of predaceous insects are specialized either for catching food on the surface or underwater.

The most conspicuous aspect of invertebrate life associated with marshes is the myriad of insects that we consider both a nuisance and, at times, a serious problem. Without a doubt, the most abundant group are the true flies, the Diptera, which include midges, mosquitoes, and crane flies. The aquatic larvae of mosquitoes occur on the surface of shallow edges and are eaten by fish, frogs, and other invertebrates. Because mosquitoes do breed in the shallow waters at the edge of marshes, and most people experience only this edge, marshes have an undeserved reputation for being unbearable because of the abundance of mosquitoes. Depending on the area and the species involved, wet meadows, oxbow swamps, and wet forest are far more important mosquito production sites. This misinterpretation is perpetuated by misidentification of marsh flies (midges) as mosquitoes. This large family of insects is one of the most important in the marsh system, at least in the North Central region. The adults swarm in unbelievable numbers and can be photographed in giant swarms against the setting sun. As is true of many marsh organisms, it is perhaps the generally unseen larvae of the midges that do most to support the system. Because of their rich red color, these are

Swarms of midges over the beach ridge of the Delta Marsh at sunset, Delta, Manitoba.

called "bloodworms"; they are found submerged in bottom soils and organic debris, serving as food for fish, frogs, and diving birds. When pupae surface and emerge as adults, they are exploited as well by surface feeding birds and fish. Swallows, ducks, terns, and small gulls like the Franklin's gull eat continuously without seeming to dent the numbers.

Mayflies occur in deeper marshes and leave their abundant cases floating on the surface as they fly away; their swimming larvae are abundant and rich food resources. The larger dragonflies and damselflies are characteristic sights of the marsh—the adults darting here and there, stopping so close, yet too fast to touch or catch. The larger dragonfly nymphs go through many growth stages (naiads) and require one to four years for maturation. Hence, they are expected only in the more permanent waters. The true bugs (Hemiptera) are represented by forms as diverse as water striders that flit about on the surface tension of the water and the predaceous backswimmers with prominent eyes and enlarged, oarlike legs. They may occur on the marsh bottom and come to the surface "belly up" for air, which is then carried with them externally. The most impressive "bugs" are the giant water bugs that may be nearly three inches long; these bugs prey on tadpoles and small fish. Also well known are the water boatmen that, though they swim with darting movements like predators, tend to eat fine algae and bottom debris. They dart to the surface for air, which is carried down to the bottom where they cling to plants.

Early summer on the marsh can produce hordes of mothlike caddis flies. Many of their larvae build cases of bits of vegetation, other organic materials, or sand. The larvae are a choice food item for some ducks, which seem to be able to extract the larvae without eating the cases. A number of aquatic beetles occur, the best known being the predaceous diving beetles, some of which are nearly two inches long. But many species exist, and their larvae are abundant on the bottom or in submerged vegetation. Better-known beetles are the "whirlygigs," which occur in colonies at the surface, moving together in sweeping circles and scattering at the slightest disturbance.

Among the most prominent of invertebrates are the crustaceans, which can be encountered even in food-poor marshes. Many of these are tiny drifting or free-swimming forms termed *plankton*; these include the water fleas such as Daphnia and the copepods such as Cyclops that challenge the unaided eye for identification. All are vital to the efficiency of food chains, for these are the animals that tap the superabundant algae and protozoans of still smaller sizes. The larger, more mobile fairy shrimp can dominate wetlands of a more temporary nature during cooler times of year, and constitute important food resources for fish, amphibians, and birds with efficient straining bills. Like insects, many crustaceans are associated with the larger submerged aquatic plants that provide food, substrate, and protection from predators.[116, 176] Examples of these crustaceans are the scuds or sideswimmers and some species of water fleas.[165] The minute seed shrimp or ostracods may use such vegetation but also are found in decaying vegetation and bottom mud.[161] Other bottom dwelling crustaceans are the aquatic sow bugs and several species of crayfish. The latter are large crustaceans that exploit various habitats and ingest both plant and animal foods. Most are bottom, or *benthic*, forms, and the shoreward species build conspicuous mud tubes from their underwater burrows. Crayfish suffer heavy predation from mink and raccoons; the aquatic forms are used by predaceous fish.

Snails and other mollusks can be extremely abundant organisms in most marshes, and are mainstays in the diet of many vertebrates.

Fingernail clams can be superabundant in silty areas, but seem more common in open, river pools and lakes than in marshes. One study on a Mississippi River pool reported 40,000 fingernail clams per square meter![70]

In addition to their use as food[179] and their conversion of plant materials to animal protein, the most essential role that invertebrates play in the system is as shredders and detritivores, which break down plant material to a size and structure where bacteria and aquatic fungi can further process these products. In the absence of these detritivores, the one-way production line would stop when all nutrients were tied up in organic material that could not be recycled. This happens in cold, acid, or polluted areas when decomposition does not keep pace with production potential—and sterile conditions result.

CHAPTER 7
Habitat Dynamics

Seasonality and Wildlife Responses to It

Perhaps the most dramatic form of habitat change, seasonality, is so common that we take it for granted. Seasonal change is especially conspicuous at high latitudes (both far north and far south), cold being the dominant physical force. But where seasonality of precipitation is great, it can be just as important in habitat change as is cold. Often, the two are interrelated.

Our studies of tundra wetlands (only part of which can be termed emergent wetlands) documented the extreme case of seasonal habitat variation, where only about 25 species of wetland birds breed in the short summer season and a few more occur in the uplands.[20] All but two upland species, willow ptarmigan and snowy owl, move out during the bleak winter, and lemming availability determines whether owls stay or not. The same phenomenon occurs in the Prairie Potholes of North Dakota and in Minnesota or Iowa marshes, except that the fauna is larger in summer. In one North Dakota marsh, 37 species nested during the summer.[114] Pheasants, horned larks, and a small number of woodland birds remained in the uplands throughout the winter. Moreover, a still larger number of migrants use these marshes during their annual stopovers.

Obviously, a warm-climate marsh need not experience this kind of seasonal change, yet changes do occur, owing to annual cycles of water availability, plant growth, insect production, and use of the marsh by mobile birds. In one study of bird species using a southern wetland (Louisiana), breeding birds numbered only 7 species, but 17 wintering species occurred.[156] During spring and fall, there were many more migrants. Breeding birds are tied to a marsh; hence, conditions there may restrict breeding. But flocks in the nonbreeding season are mobile and can utilize diverse foods where they are most readily found.[26] Such adaptability not only is energy efficient, but maintains the maximal population of a species.

Like other birds, most marsh birds return in the spring to nest in last year's vegetation, but if this vegetation is missing for some reason, most birds probably simply look elsewhere. However, in several years of observation in the marshes of Northwest Iowa, it became apparent that members of some species, yellow-headed blackbirds and coots, remained in flocks in the marsh and nested later, when new plant growth appeared. Some of this behavior may be due to late migration by young birds, but habitat conditions also play a major role. Characteristically, yellow-headed blackbirds' nests are made of dead cattail leaves woven on old stalks, whereas these late-nesters attached them to green shoots. Often one shoot grows faster than another, causing the nest to pitch over and the eggs or young to fall out. We suspect from color patterns that these birds are yearling females that nest late and probably are less successful. The pattern in coots also needs additional study, but young birds do seem to nest later than adults. Moreover, late nests built of green materials seem less buoyant in heavy winds, and the nest success probably is reduced.

Although birds and a few insects react to seasonality by mobility, relatively few marsh mammals migrate. Northern muskrats survive severe winters by lodge construction and food storage plus local movement to marshes of freeze-proof depth.[59, 60] This behavior in itself limits which marshes are suitable over-wintering habitat for muskrats. A lodge is not impenetrable by a fox, but muskrats can escape underwater, making digging a probable waste of time for the predator. In times of drought, muskrats can suffer severe losses to such terrestrial predators.[61] Thus, seasonality affects what the muskrat can do and how it does it.

The effect of seasonality on truly aquatic forms is even more striking, as it causes the physical conditions to which life cycles, reproductive sites, and other biological phenomena have evolved. Annual crops are the rule, however, for the majority of marsh animals of shallow marshes, because chances are good that marsh conditions won't be the same next year. Dragonflies, salamanders, and fish that require several years to mature are associated with more permanent marshes or ponds (Type IV or V).

Succession and Other Changes

Our general concepts of natural changes in vegetation (and obviously associated animals) have been conditioned by long-term views and terrestrial systems. Ecologists understandably have been most interested in piecing together past history, especially since the ice ages. There are, as a result, a few classical studies of plant and animal communities of ponds of various ages formed along old beach ridges, or of the various stages (and ages) of pond-bog succession as seen in northern coniferous forests.[106] The texts tend to emphasize such successional trends, showing how a shallow lake eventually is filled by sediments and organic matter and becomes marshlike or boglike and eventually is grown over by the dominant local terrestrial vegetation (Fig. 3).[29] The wetland aspect of this successional sequence is of importance here. Lakes that are clear and deep tend to be low in productivity (*oligotrophic*);[168] they become sedimented, less clear, enriched with nutrients, and higher in basic productivity (*eutrophic*) as part of the succession created by natural filling with rich soils and organic matter. The rate of such eutrophication depends on many factors of the surrounding uplands, as well as the depth of the wetland, the nutrient base stemming from its substrate, the rate of inflow and sedimentation, the climatic regime, and so on.[126] These aspects of long-term succession also are factors in short-term changes, with which we are most concerned here.

Animal succession associated with long-term plant and water quality changes is reflected in the different stages from pond to grown-over marsh or bog. Thus, the deep and clear pond may contain fish that favor clear water, open-water birds, such as loons, that feed on fish, and invertebrates that require relative permanence. Later phases include the dense submergent stage with floating-leaf vegetation, marsh-loving birds, and invertebrates influenced by an abundance of detritus. Finally, the moist terrestrial vegetation in the final seral stage demonstrates an animal fauna similar to that of the uplands.[29]

Although this general trend may be true over thousands of years, it may not always occur, and it may not be a simple one-directional successional pattern.[137] There may be periodic reversals toward deeper water, or to drought or drainage that suddenly produces terrestrial conditions. The trends

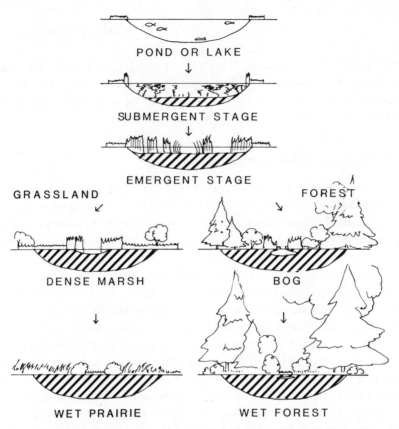

Figure 3. *Theoretical long-term succession from pond or lake, through the emergent marsh stage, to local climax terrestrial vegetation. Because of natural deepening processes, this might involve thousands or even tens of thousands of years.*

as well as the habitats are dynamic, forcing animal residents to be equally responsive—or move—or die.

This concept is based on the theory of directional and almost predetermined long-term change in plant communities toward a climatically controlled "climax" vegetation of Clements.[39a] Current concepts of marsh succession[212a] are based more on Gleason's concepts[74a] of site variation, randomness, and plant life history strategies with water as the major driving force. This concept better explains the observations of short-term change that we see during drought-produced drawdowns in wetlands.

Because they have been less emphasized in textbooks, because they are more visible in a short-term time frame of three to ten years, and because they dramatically affect the wildlife of any discrete marsh unit, I want to detail some of the kinds of short-term vegetative change and wildlife-induced changes, as well as wildlife responses

to these changes. My comments are based on: (1) observational studies, wherein descriptions are made[46] on one area annually for several
years to document changes that infer successional patterns;[226, 227]
and (2) experimental studies, in which water level manipulations
were used to recreate these stages and demonstrate causal factors.[225]
Some general concepts will set the stage for appreciating the dynamics of wildlife populations, the human influences on wetlands, and
the necessity of management strategies.

Two forces dramatically influence change in marsh vegetation and
the associated animal communities. The most crucial is changing
water depth, which, as indicated earlier, is the deciding influence on
what plants grow where and what plant life forms (i.e., emergents or
floating-leaf) dominate a particular marsh. Changing water levels also
create stress for established plants, with deep water reducing the
growth of even well-adapted emergents, and shallow water (and especially dryness) reducing growth of all but the wet-meadow or edge
species. Thus, vegetative growth and plant distributions are dynamic,
with rapid spread in some years and reduced growth or even dieback
in others.

The second major influence on marsh vegetation is a product of
the activity of herbivores such as muskrats,[62] (introduced) nutria, or
occasionally beavers that "eat out" large areas of vegetation used for
lodges and food. Because of the physiological nature of most emergent plants, such cuttings will not regrow if they are flooded by even
an inch of water—and they die in a year or so for lack of oxygen in
spite of much stored food resources in the rhizomes and tubers.[148, 222]
If such cuttings are not inundated, or if the water level actually
declines, regrowth is usual—though not always with the same density
or robustness, since their photosynthetic ability is reduced and spring
growth is based initially in nutrients stored in rootstocks.

Because water levels are usually a direct response to rainfall, and
since rainfall patterns vary year-to-year and geographically, changes
in marsh water levels are common in the prairie pothole regions[107, 209]
and occasionally occur even in more stable climates in the northern
and eastern forests. The interaction of these two forces thereby influences the vegetation and the wildlife of single marshes or even of
marshes of major geographic regions. Whole areas may be dominated
by wetlands in a certain condition: All may be shallow and meadowlike or may be flooded and semi-open. Depending on the variety of

sizes and depths of marshes in an area, major shifts in birds must occur between wetlands and regions, but let us first examine a typical pattern in a midwestern marsh.

Short-Term Vegetational Changes. If an open marsh or shallow lake goes dry, the bottom sediments are exposed. Organic debris that has settled in the water for several to many years dries and decomposes through the action of invertebrates, fungi, and bacteria; invertebrates, turtles, and fish die and decompose; toxic substances stored under reduced oxygen conditions deteriorate.[41] Soil structure is modified by alternate wetting and drying, and, finally, cracking deep into the substrate layer. In some cases, soil may be blown from the basin, deepening it. In other cases, it may form a catch basin for new and rich soil blown across the prairies or fields from unvegetated uplands.[1] Obviously, the substrate is different, and, in most cases, it is probably a better site for plant growth, because nutrients are in a more usable form.

Surprisingly, most marsh emergents are not sufficiently well adapted to water that their seeds will germinate in deep water. In fact, some either won't germinate at all or are very specific in relation to oxygen levels, temperature, and so on, so the cracked but wet and muddy bottom of a marsh is a superb seed bed for the marsh edge plants like sedges, softstem bulrush, moisture-loving grasses, arrowhead, willow and cottonwood trees (which can be a serious problem in drawdowns), and even the deeper water plants such as hardstem bulrush and cattail.[139, 225] Such dry conditions are not suitable for the submergents like sago pondweed or water lilies, which do germinate underwater. Thousands of seeds survive in a dormant condition on the marsh bottom and, even in the center of a marsh where such plants haven't grown for 5 to 15 years, buried seeds of marsh plants will suddenly germinate.[22, 44, 77, 187, 188] (Marsh ecologists term these residual seeds the "seed bank."[213]) Thus, the entire exposed marsh bottom may be green with tiny plants that at first look very much alike. As they develop at different rates, influenced by moisture or water level and other factors,[84, 86] one finds slender, linear-leaved cattail and bulrush plants side by side with willows and sedges and other marsh-edge plants.

As water returns to the marsh, the survival, growth, and reproductive success of plants is influenced by the time of year, rate of flooding, degree of inundation, water clarity, herbivore activity, wave action, and many other influences.[99, 139, 141, 225] Most of these marsh-

A. *Oak-rimmed Rush Lake in Northwest Iowa at a dense marsh stage following drawdown and revegetation.*

B. *Bogs are usually acid lakes or pools with an overgrowing mat of mosses, sedges, cattail, shrubs, and even trees. Marsh vegetation occurs in these settings, but such wetlands usually are classified as bogs or bog lakes rather than marshes.*

C. *Typical Prairie Pothole country near Roseneath, Manitoba. Drainage and filling are gradually eliminating these extensive wetland complexes.*[107]

D. *Arrowhead or Duck Potato is a common wet-soil or shallow marsh plant that produces rich tubers eaten by ducks and muskrats.*

E. *A natural wetland overfertilized by livestock wastes with a resultant bloom of floating duckweed. The effects of grazing on vegetation are evident.*

F. *Hardstem bulrush is among the most water tolerant of the emergent plants, persisting in shallow lakes as well as the deeper sections of marshes. However, because of its effective root system, it can be equally tolerant of drought.*

G. *Yellow water lily is a floating-leaf plant common to deep marshes and shallow lakes. These leaves, like branches of a spreading tree, tap sunlight over a large area and store nutrients in huge rootstocks that supply the initial thrust of the next season's growth.*

H. *A pair of Forster's terns at a nest on a muskrat house in a stand of cattail. Nest success usually is quite high at such sites.*

I. *Female least bittern on the nest showing the "freeze" position for which bitterns are so well known. This inconspicuous bird can be extremely common but is unknown to passersby who do not penetrate the cattail and bulrush of the deep marsh.*

J. *The prairie marsh in winter with muskrat lodges protruding through the snow and ice. Most birds are gone but muskrats are active underwater, and mink and weasels are active the year around.*

K. *Fire in marshes is dangerous during the breeding period because of the losses to nesting waterbirds. However, winter burns may be useful in opening dense vegetation, recharging the nutrient base, and stimulating certain types of vegetation.*

L. *A Waterfowl Production Area in the more rugged North Dakota "Coteau." Such "WPAs" are owned or leased by the U.S. Fish and Wildlife Service and managed for wildlife production. Hunting normally is permitted, but disturbance should be minimized during the breeding season. This is a Type IV wetland in the open phase, showing diverse emergent plants along the edge and sparse hardstem bulrush "islands" in the central marsh. Water depths typically range from 1.5 to 3.5 feet.*

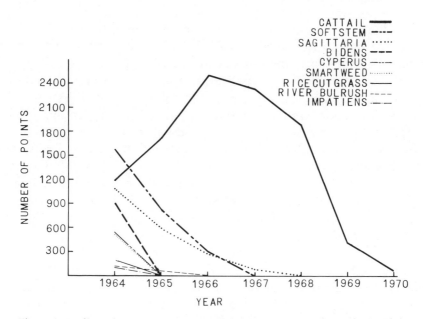

Figure 4. *Decline of wet-meadow and mud-flat species concurrent with growth in abundance of cattail.*[225] *Following reflooding, wet-meadow species such as beggarstick (Bidens) and smartweed were eliminated in one or two years. Marsh-edge species like arrowhead and softstem bulrush survived two to four years of flooding, whereas cattail increased for several years until it was eaten out by muskrats or floated up by high water.*

edge plants are water-tolerant enough that they survive from one to three years (Fig. 4), but the better adapted deep-marsh plants like cattail outcompete other species in the deeper water depths.[225] Gradually, the plant species composition of the wetland is set by its new average water depth as related to the germination history during drawdown and reflooding. Submergent plants probably germinate at the shallow water depths and may not become conspicuous for several years. Because different species of submergents also are adapted to different water conditions, those like sago that favor shallow depths suffer under high water conditions.

With higher water, marshes gradually open. Part of this opening is due to herbivores (to be discussed next), but much vegetative loss occurs also because of the buoyancy of tubers of cattail and water lilies, which store larger quantities of food. (These tubers are so rich in nutrients that American Indians used them as food.) As muskrats dig out tubers, and as carp and other fish root around the bottom oozes, they disrupt such plants, which float to the surface. Even large clumps of cattail may be seen floating around the marsh, moved by the winds; in some places, lodged plants may establish new root systems and stabilize open shores. Just as the species composition of marsh plants generally increases as one traces the history of pond-to-marsh development in any series, the reflooding of a dry lake or marsh basin reverses that pattern over a period of three to five years. A tally of germinated plants on the mud flat might show virtually all the species common to all depths of a marsh, but these gradually are reduced to a few water-adapted species; and one or two dominants such as cattail, hardstem bulrush, or reed may be the only vegetation present after several years (Fig. 4). This decline in species richness seems unique, for in most plant communities, the tendency is for the variety of plants to increase.

Muskrat Populations. Drought virtually eliminates muskrats from marshes.[60, 61] Some emigrate, as is obvious from mortality on highways; some are eaten by foxes and mink as they try to persist in submarginal habitat; and reproduction all but ceases. It doesn't take long for them to return, however, when water returns to the marsh. The vegetative growth is explosive (and probably highly nutritious), and they may move in during summer even though the water depths are insufficient for winter. Their small numbers are hardly noticeable from the shore, and the first winter after flooding may show few lodges. But muskrats are microtine rodents like meadow mice, and their capacity for reproduction is impressive. They can have four litters per year with six or more young each time, and even their early young may produce a litter their first year when food is good and competition is reduced.[60] Exponential growth is the rule at this stage and in several years, populations may increase manyfold (Fig. 5).[225] This explosive growth has a bearing both on the marsh system and on management, which we'll consider later.

In the marsh system, the burst of herbivores means that plant growth may be eaten as rapidly as it is produced. There are two major uses: Food resources are selected carefully and their removal is perceptible only as one canoes through a marsh and finds entire platforms made of criss-crossed plants. The more edible parts (rootstocks, rhizomes, and tips) may be removed and the harder and older stems are used as a platform and left to rot. But the most dramatic removal takes place in late summer, when vast areas may be cut to build lodges that must survive the winter and which the muskrats must have for protection from weather and predators. The construc-tion of lodges in this early stage of the marsh reestablishment is an especially interesting phenomenon for, either because of reduced competition or because of the robust growth of dominant plants at this stage, lodges may be 6 feet high and 15 feet in diameter, whereas they are half that size later, when populations are high and materials are less abundant. Such cutting comes so quickly that the opening of

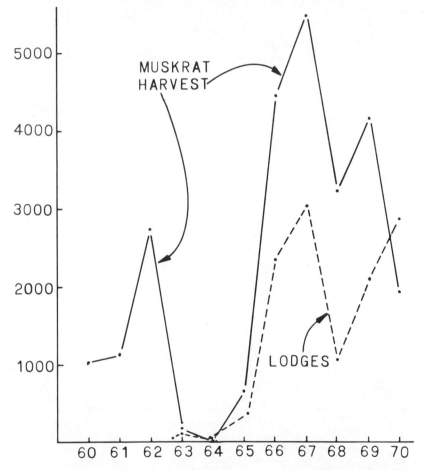

Figure 5. *Muskrat populations may literally explode after the reflooding of suitable dense emergent cover such as cattail. This example from Rush Lake in Iowa shows the harvest of muskrats that increased from 640 in 1965 following reflooding, to 5,509 in 1967.*[225] *In this isolated marsh, few remained after drawdowns in 1964 and, even with immigration, reproductive rate must have been phenomenal. This is a harvest of about 14 muskrats per acre, and probably represented only 50 to 60 percent of the total resident population.*

even a dense marsh can occur in a few weeks. Thereafter, the rate of opening depends on factors that influence muskrat reproduction and over-wintering success. Reproduction slows when populations climb, by virtue of reduced litter size, reduced number of litters per year, and reduced survival of the young.

Such populations can build to a point that they strip the marsh.[62, 226] Dependent on the basin shape, this stripping usually occurs in the center first, since muskrats seek the deeper depths where they are less vulnerable. If water levels rise, muskrats move

Cattail seeds by the tens of thousands drift from each head. Germination of seeds may be very high on suitable mud flats but cattail also spreads continuously by vegetative propagation.

Revegetation of Rush Lake near Ayeshire, Iowa, after a muskrat eat-out. Partial (top) and complete (middle) drawdown resulted in germination of dormant seeds that had been underwater, and and produced an excellent stand of emergent vegetation attractive to a variety of birds (bottom). Openings of this size and variety rarely occur during the first year, but the wetland usually is not attractive to birds until they develop.

A muskrat feeding platform is built of leafy remains of cattail after the tuberous base has been eaten.

shoreward and strip even that. Sometimes they leave the marsh to feed in wet meadows or cornfields, leaving little food anywhere. A population crash is inevitable. If, on the other hand, water levels decline, the vegetation may be saved, but the muskrats must move out of the marsh for lack of suitable over-wintering depth. If water levels decline during winter, muskrats are forced to move at a vulnerable time, and high mortality results.[61] Trapping can accomplish the same thing on small areas and is an important management tool. Other factors relative to nutrition may influence slowing of population growth. The world-renowned specialist, Paul Errington, long felt that there were unexplained population phenomena, wherein muskrats were more productive at some times than others.

Impact of Vegetation Changes on Bird Populations. From the general descriptions of both the kinds of habitats various birds use, and their species-specific adaptability, it is obvious that some bird species respond to slight changes in habitat. Vegetation patterns and structure seem to be the major visual clue to which marsh birds respond initially. Undoubtedly, food must be present next, and at a density

Two views of Goose or Anderson Lake near Jewell, Iowa. Upper photo shows the dense emergent vegetation that occurred in summer of 1959; lower shows the lakelike conditioning following a muskrat eat-out in 1962.

that minimizes time wasted in foraging. For breeding birds, nest sites must be present, and our data on the usual sites selected gives a quantitative measure of what is used (but it is difficult to relate to what is not used). We gain further insights into preference as we observe changes from year to year. Thus, yellow-headed blackbirds that nest over water may return to their breeding marsh of a previous year to find that muskrats have stripped much of last year's cover. The marsh is relatively unattractive to the birds unless emergent vegetation is standing in water. Some birds may battle for the few remaining sites, but others abandon them to the redwings, which tolerate lower, less robust, and more open cover. Even the redwing males may find the habitat less attractive to females and eventually abandon their territories.[226]

If, however, muskrats have simply cut openings in otherwise dense vegetation, the visual stimulus is attractive to both species of blackbirds. The redwings, arriving first, set up territories along their favored edges but also move well out into the marsh. As the yellow-headed blackbirds arrive, brief battles ensue, but within a few days redwings are displaced into the edge or into habitat less attractive to yellow-heads—even if it is far from shore.[226, 231] In all probability, territory placement, harem size, social encounters, and reproductive success are influenced by habitat change.

Nest-site selection of Forster's and black terns show even more specific association with a microhabitat. In general, black terns will use either very small marshes or small openings in large marshes. Their manner of flight and their adeptness at feeding on invertebrates at the water's surface makes this behavior practical. Forster's terns are fish feeders, however, and generally are associated with larger marshes or lake edges or very large pools in larger marshes. But nest site selection is rather species-specific, with Forster's terns using large, dry muskrat lodges (or other dry sites) whereas black terns select low, deteriorating lodges (or build soggy sites of wet vegetation). Thus, black terns may move in immediately after flooding, using sites created by flooding of sedges and other low, wet-meadow plants. Forster's terns are prevalent in the mid-stages of the reflooding, when large lodges have been built but only after large pools of open water are present. Hence, habitat change creates a shift not only in spatial distribution but also in bird species richness and numbers (Fig. 6).[225] Figure 7 summarizes these patterns of change.[226]

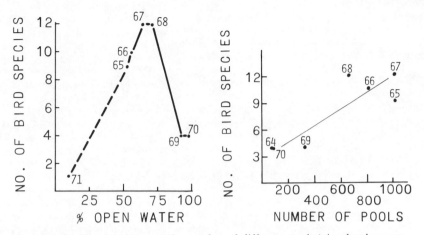

Figure 6. *Bird species richness (the number of different species) is related to area (percent) of open water and the interspersion of open water in dense cover. These examples suggest that the highest number of species occurred with 50-75 percent open water and the maximal number of small pools in dense emergents.*[225] *The figures may vary from area to area dependent on plant life form, species composition, and the nearness of other wetlands, but structural features of this type are clearly important in attracting birds.*

■ WATER ▨ CATTAIL ▦ HARDSTEM			
WATER DEPTH	SHALLOW	MEDIUM	DEEP
VEGETATION	DENSE	MODERATE	SPARSE
BIRD POPULATIONS	NUMEROUS INDIV.	MANY INDIV.	FEW INDIV.
BIRD SPECIES RICHNESS	FEW KINDS	MANY KINDS	FEW KINDS
MUSKRATS	FEW	MANY	FEW

Figure 7. *As a marsh passes from dense vegetation to open water because of the action of high water and muskrat activity, considerable change takes place in the numbers of muskrats and birds, and a major change in bird-species richness. The same pattern of animal numbers and species richness is characteristic of wetlands that remain in these structural conditions for long periods owing to water regimes.*

After reestablishment of dense stands of emergents following drawdowns, muskrats slowly invade and build lodges, creating small openings. As further vegetation is cut or eaten, and these pools increase in size, the area becomes most attractive to the greatest variety and the largest numbers of birds.

The extreme cases of habitat change do bring about the elimination of some species. When bottom soils are dry and weed-covered, pheasants, meadowlarks, and mourning doves nest on the ground.[226] Song sparrows and other upland passerines may nest in low shrubs or trees. When water levels are too low, waterfowl simply do not stop[115] and some move long distances to nest;[192] some stop but do not nest.[173] When reflooded, the same vegetation might be used by a variety of semiaquatic species before the development of other, more aquatic, plants. In such situations, yellow-headed blackbirds, coots, or canvasbacks may nest in willows when they are flooded.

Some adaptable species like coots and pied-billed grebes are tolerant of a wide range of vegetation, as long as foods and nesting material are present and water depth is adequate for swimming. Both species require some small openings in dense vegetation, and favor semi-open conditions, but are tolerant of rather open situations in which their nests are totally exposed—as long as they have nest material. Emergent cover as such is not necessary, but their nests must be protected by old stubs of emergent plants or, occasionally, dense beds of submergents near the surface that keep wave action from destroying the nest. Only wide open lake conditions eventually discourage breeding birds from returning. Eared grebe colonies often occur in wide open but shallow lakes, where the birds build nests in and of submergents that are at water level and that protect the nests from wind damage.

Figure 8 diagrams these general influences on bird species and population changes from dry to wet cycles, and from dense to open vegetation.

The Importance of Food Resources

Birds and other wildlife species feed heavily on insect and other animal matter, which is most abundant during the summer (Fig.

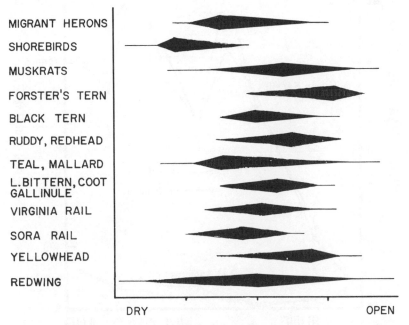

Figure 8. *This schematic diagram shows the influence of habitat selection on bird species composition of a wetland.*[226] *Some species like shorebirds and waders occur only during the "damp" stages, whereas redhead and ruddy ducks favor the deep-open stage.*

9)[20, 47, 92, 202] and which may be the greatest attraction of the marsh. All too little has been written on how invertebrates,[179] frogs, and other food resources in marshes are related to vegetative zone or marsh type. Hence, it is more difficult to assess the effect of water-level changes and vegetation changes on these animals. One of my former graduate students has gathered data on some dominant wetland types, formulating a simple model of what would happen with change in marsh type from newly germinated areas to those opened by high water and muskrats (Fig. 10).[217] These data suggest that major changes in invertebrate species and numbers do occur and that

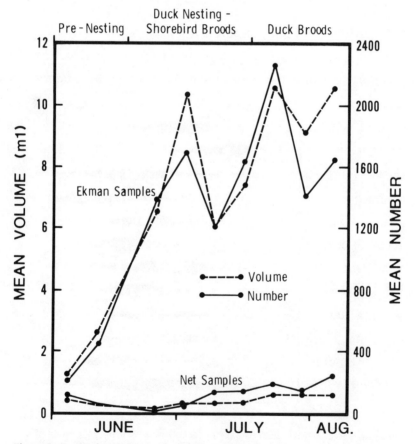

Figure 9. *Seasonal variation in the bottom (Ekman dredge samples) and planktonic (net) invertebrates of some Alaskan tundra ponds, showing peak numbers and volume in July, when duck and shorebird numbers are at their peak.*[20]

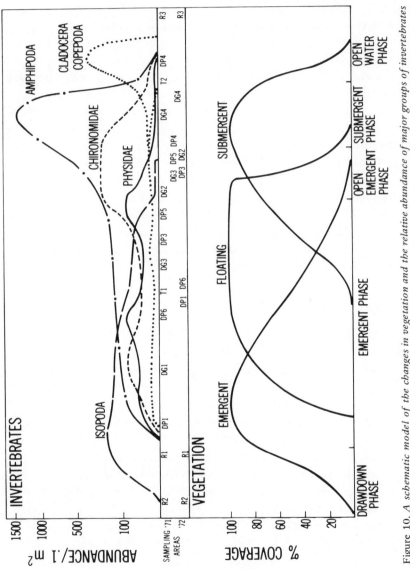

Figure 10. A schematic model of the changes in vegetation and the relative abundance of major groups of invertebrates in a prairie wetland. This figure was constructed by Voigts (1976), according to observations of populations and conditions in several different wetlands. [217] Its value may not be so much its precise accuracy for any single wetland as a demonstration of the dynamics of its vegetation and invertebrates.

they could have a major influence on birds that use the area. For example, plankton are abundant when vegetation is decomposing and nutrients are being returned to the aquatic system.[217] Shovelers have bills highly specialized for straining plankton, a food resource commonly used by fish and other aquatic animals. It is not unusual to see a pair of shovelers on any small wetland, but large flocks (in spring migration or post-breeding) are common on open marshes where few other ducks occur and where foods would seem scarce. They are there for the plankton.

Diving ducks dependent on snails or on bottom-dwelling midge larvae also may occur in open marsh types, but other marsh stages are more productive of even these organisms and, therefore, of these ducks. Dabbling ducks like blue-winged teal that feed on snails and other invertebrates in more shallow, densely vegetated areas shift to larger wetlands during drawdown phases in open marshes, showing both flexibility and adaptability to rich resources.[203] Recent data from both observational and experimental studies suggest strongly that these invertebrate resources are the major influence on water-bird use and production in marshes.[19, 57, 98, 103]

The Importance of Instability

Most current evidence shows that stabilizing water at high levels is detrimental to marshes because it tends to create lakelike situations, where production is aquatic rather than semiaquatic. Organic production in emergent plants is reduced, as deep water favors submergents or pad-plants. Invertebrate production probably is less, especially of detritivores, and total nutrient availability probably is lower. Toxic substances may build up under the anaerobic conditions of continuous flooding,[41] and the return of nitrogen and phosphorus to the system may be slowed.[100] At low levels, marshes become too dense and more like terrestrial systems. But periodic drying and reflooding is generally beneficial. This need for seasonal instability, though, should not be interpreted as a need for erratic water level changes at any time of the year. Fluctuations that are too rapid may cause mortality of muskrats[38] and ducks[90] if it occurs during the breeding period. Some mortality will occur, and further research is needed to evaluate long-term gains versus short-term losses.

CHAPTER 8
Management and Restoration

Philosophical Considerations

To manage or not to manage—this controversial issue in resource conservation stems from a new public awareness of environmental issues and activities. The opinions are, unfortunately, strongly divided, but the reasons for the philosophical difference seem at times unrelated to the wildlife resource. Rather than review the arguments on either side of this issue, it seems more profitable here to clarify some goals and then discuss methods for achieving them.

In view of the extensive loss of wetlands in North America and around the world, our major emphasis must be to conserve marshes as communities in a natural state for present and future generations. In many cases, this policy will mean only acquisition and protection (a form of management) but, in some cases, human modification or manipulation will be valuable, if not essential. I suggest that our national policy include the preservation of wetland complexes in as typical a natural state as possible. This action might involve purchase, in a balanced pattern, of representatives of all typical wetland classes in an area, or, where this is impossible, management of some more abundant types to stages comparable to those lost. This procedure will help maintain faunal and floral diversity typical of that region and avoid endangering some species while overproducing others. This approach is, of course, more problematic than the preservation of a single wetland or of the management of that unit; it requires a recognition that: (1) wetlands serve more mobile species like birds as a complex,[224] and (2) that the modification of one wetland influences others nearby.

A general philosophy of management might be to leave well enough alone when a wetland is in a natural state and seems productive, but use natural techniques when man-influenced wetlands are not productive. Moreover, when management is deemed necessary, we must understand that a marsh is a complex system and must be managed as such. Management goals must consider all species, not single ones or small groups; most changed conditions affect all organisms.

To reduce excessive, often unnecessary, and overly artificial management programs, goals should emphasize: (1) long-term productivity, under the most natural conditions possible, by maintaining natural values through the use of natural processes; (2) long-term over short-term benefits; and (3) conservation programs that serve the greatest range of public interests.[223] Conservation agencies, however, may take different attitudes toward management needs and techniques, dependent on whether they serve the wildlife resource or a user clientele.[23] Both must be considered concurrently, but some user regulation is necessary to avoid permanent damage to wildlife habitat.

Situations that may encourage management are those extreme stages of succession that seem to cause wildlife to reduce their use of marshes. Excessive water from modified drainage systems creates lakelike environments. Because revegetation is essentially restricted to drawdown conditions, several methods may be used to achieve the germination phase, but those that have their basis in natural events are preferred. Inflow modifications rather than outlet structures may be more effective, and may, indeed, be necessary. Increased eutrophication, at either open or dense stages, could be a product of pollution with excessive nutrients. Management to correct the problem might involve upstream impoundment or changes in watershed cover plants, but too little is known as yet, either of the problem or its solution.

The opposite extreme is vegetation so dense that birds are not attracted. This condition is more difficult to assess and to control, but even songbirds seem to have a preference for patchy as opposed to continuous cover; open water seems to be a vital ingredient.[226] The opening of this dense cover adds a diversity of plant life, and presumably invertebrates, and encourages bird use. In large marshes, we have found that a 50:50 cover:water ratio is ideal,[225, 226] but diversity can come from several small marshes in different stages. Regardless of the specific goal, several options are available for creating this diversity.

Acquisition of Wetlands

The purchase of marshes and other wetlands as wildlife refuges is well known, having been the only feasible way of protecting unique areas for bird nesting colonies or as strategic migration stops. The Audubon Society, and U.S. Fish and Wildlife Service, Ducks Unlimited, The Nature Conservancy, and numerous state and local conservation agencies have thus acquired significant acreages of marshes.

Since the early 1960s, the U.S. Fish and Wildlife Service has been acquiring Waterfowl Production Areas ("WPA"s) to help maintain continental production of waterfowl and other migratory birds. All are purchases or leases made via funds already acquired or borrowed against future purchases by duck hunters of federal duck stamps required to hunt waterfowl. These funds totaled nearly $200 million by 1979. In North Dakota, nearly 1 million acres have been purchased or leased as of 1980.[129] The WPA program has run into serious difficulty, however, because of local and state opposition to taking land out of the tax base, objections to increased federally owned land and federal influence in state issues, and increased limitations on deeds that would limit property resale. In addition to the special goal of buying wetlands, these funds have purchased some beautiful wet prairie and uplands in the Prairie Pothole Region that will serve wider audiences than duck hunters. In addition, The Nature Conservancy and some private foundations have conserved wetlands with the intent of preserving unique, representative, natural communities as part of our national heritage. Their acquisitions tend to preserve all forms of typical wetlands, regardless of their wildlife values. In addition, such organizations often perform a unique service in helping government agencies in purchase since they can act more quickly and can hold property until other action can be taken.

Natural Methods: Water Level Regulation

The use of natural forces and processes in management is most likely to stimulate natural events, conditions, and results.[3] In most cases, these techniques are the least expensive to use and have the greatest permanence. As mentioned earlier regarding the dynamic changes in marshes, the dominant forces are water level fluctuation, herbivore utilization of plant materials, ice action, and possibly fire and nutrient turnover.

Water level management is generally only feasible when a water control structure has been constructed to either restore a marsh or to aid in water level stability. Whether such structures should be added to a natural marsh to provide water level control is a debatable question for which there can be no universal answer. In some cases, the success of management may justify the effort. In others, the area may require it because of modified stream flow, lowered water tables, increased sedimentation due to wind or water erosion, increased disturbance or consumption of vegetation because of artificially high levels of wildlife or domestic livestock, and so forth. Massive dams usually are unnecessary, excessively expensive, and no more functional than smaller ones.[13] Low earthern structures can be built that differ little from natural "glacial walls" but that effectively impede drainage.

Conflict has been common between biologists, who want to design management systems to maximize biological productivity, and engineers, who wish to devise water management systems. Communication between the two groups often has been poor or lacking, and the outcome sometimes disastrous for wildlife. Engineers can design suitable water management systems for marsh management only if they first understand the biological goals of management, and the sensitivity of the marsh community to water fluctuations. Overengineered structures tend to lack the sophisticated controls essential for good marsh management. A common failing is a control structure that cannot regulate levels within the necessary precision of two or three inches. Another weakness is the siteing of the control structure in such a way that periodic complete drainage of the basin, an essential device for creating suitable plant seed beds or eliminating carp or muskrats, is impossible.

Water level control through pumping out water or pumping in

water has been exercised commonly, but it is expensive in equipment, time, and operational costs. However, the process and the results are natural; the decision to use this procedure is a judgment that must be made in light of other possible options or potential pressures for misuse of the system.

Regardless of how water level regulation is accomplished, it may be used to flood out dense vegetation established during dry periods, or to dry out the marsh for revegetation. Drawdowns for revegetation may be: (A) *complete*, when major restoration is essential in an open marsh; or (B) *partial*, when vegetation needs to be encouraged or herbivores discouraged:

A. Complete drawdowns are common when all central vegetation has been lost owing to muskrat eat-outs; high water levels, often in combination with excessive carp populations; winter kill; and occasionally plant disease. Procedures are as follows: [123, 223]

1. Lowering water levels permits the germination of naturally occurring seed and the recovery of established but flood-stressed emergents and even submergents. Although collecting, growing, and planting of seeds and tubers once was common,[118] natural supplies usually are adequate.

2. The degree of drawdown depends on the basin shape and water availability, but decomposition of bottom vegetation and cracking of bottom muds is ideal for most plants.

3. The length of drawdown is uncertain, but drying of the soil and breakdown of vegetation to release bound nutrients may require most of the growing season. Over-winter drawdowns often have proved effective. In certain settings, late fall or early winter (post-hunting) drawdowns can be left until reflooding in late summer (pre-hunting), so that duck hunting is not seriously affected. Muskrats will be drastically reduced over winter, however, which may be desirable for marsh management but less popular for muskrat trappers. Timing of the drawdown may be used to make trapping more successful and satisfy both user groups.

4. Reflooding should be a gradual process, to avoid flotation of emergents, direct scouring of other plants, or plant mortality due to the turbidity of muddy waters. Late summer flooding may induce muskrat use if depths are freeze-proof in northern

latitudes. Keeping water levels low may attract birds but will not attract muskrats.

5. Water levels should be regulated mainly for vegetation growth, diversity, and survival during the second (first reflooded) season, as long-term trends demonstrate a gradual decline of emergent vegetation with stable or high water levels (Fig. 11). Some concern for wildlife must be deferred at this time, since long-term production of wildlife will be enhanced in later seasons.

6. Subsequently, marsh management for the benefit of wildlife will consider welfare of the vegetation, but manipulation will be designed mainly to regulate muskrat use[223] and enhance bird use.[180] Knowledge of species requirements is essential, but the "system" will be self-forming and dynamic.

7. Some submergents may germinate on mud flats, but most germinate underwater because they are better adapted to aquatic conditions. Excessive depths, however, especially of turbid water, are detrimental to submergents.

8. After several years, reduction of muskrats or carp via late fall drawdown may conserve vegetation. Not all muskrat populations "explode," but many do, and lowered water level in-

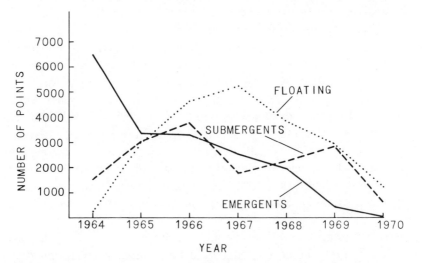

Figure 11. *A history of the three major plant life forms in Rush Lake following reflooding.*[225] *Whereas floating or submergent plants varied in number according to water levels and wave action, emergents gradually declined, owing to muskrat depredation for lodges and food.*

creases their vulnerability to traps. Carp may freeze out over winter if depths are kept shallow.

B. Partial drawdowns should be used where vegetation is seriously reduced, wildlife use has declined, or water levels have stressed vegetation.

   1. Water levels should be reduced to meadowlike depths, to encourage vegetative propagation of emergents and germination and growth of submergents in early summer, especially at the marsh perimeter. Wildlife use by species like inland diving ducks and coots that favor deep water will decline; use by waders, shorebirds, and dabbling ducks may increase markedly.

   2. This low level should be retained or even lowered in late summer, and returned to near-normal levels in early fall.

   3. It is best not to keep freeze-proof depths, except where plant density is high and muskrats are to be encouraged. The presence of carp is a consideration.

   4. As vegetation recovers, levels are regulated to allow nesting or plant consumption as desired.

Natural Methods: Herbivores and Other Vegetation Management

Management of muskrats, nutrias, beaver[29a] or other herbivores is a valuable but more difficult management tool, since it depends on the efficiency of population regulation.[34, 117] If management guidelines are flexible, trappers can effectively control muskrats and nutria where water control is lacking or limited. In most midwestern marshes, trapping too late in the population "boom" creates more problems than does overtrapping the population. Not only are muskrats difficult to trap, but unpredictable weather conditions, low fur prices that discourage trapping, and unnecessary restrictions on places and methods of trapping reduce trapping success, make population control difficult, and are detrimental to marsh management results.

The use of livestock grazing to manipulate vegetation has met with mixed reaction by wildlife managers,[109] and has been applied less commonly to marshes than to other cover types. In most cases to date, extreme overgrazing has had negative effects on duck nesting and habitat quality in uplands and marshes,[227] but we must maintain an open attitude on the use of grazing as a tool in marshes until more careful experimental data are available. After all, bison grazed the entire West and Midwest and must have exploited marsh resources at times. A herd of cattle can be devastating to a marsh, but a few wandering cattle might simulate the effects of bison and result in more attractive and accessible patchy cover for use by birds. We know that certain terrestrial species are attracted by shorter cover, as for example, the upland sandpiper. How marsh birds respond is still uncertain.

Fire has been used extensively in Gulf Coast marshes but less commonly in glacial potholes.[36, 91] Natural fires must have occurred regularly before the intervention of man, and possibly functioned, as do drawdowns, to eliminate the bulk of plant biomass and to return some major nutrients to the flow cycle. A great difficulty in using fire is that it often spreads too far, too fast, and uncontrollably. Certainly, fire can never be resorted to in a marsh during the breeding season, as disastrous results could occur when early nesting ducks explore the tinder-dry marsh vegetation of the previous years' growth.[33] Some positive benefits of burning reeds have been reported for managing marsh-edge nesting areas for dabbling ducks.[218] Fire has been used to deepen bog wetlands in some North Central states, but it is very difficult to direct and to extinguish.[123]

The release of nutrients by a fire has caused some speculation and some casual experimentation on the use of fertilizers to enrich marshes. This practice seems wasteful, since marshes seem to be nutrient "sumps" anyway, capturing and storing nitrogen and phosphorus. Release of such riches is difficult and accomplished better naturally.

Artificial Methods

Artificial seeding and planting of vegetation often was attempted during early marsh restoration efforts, for the protection of shorelines, or for waterfowl food production. Failures were common, and such efforts now are quite rare, restricted to special cases of intensive management of emergents or the large-scale production of waterfowl foods on migration stops or wintering areas. In most cases, natural seed banks seem more than adequate if water levels can be manipulated to induce germination.

Basin deepening is the most common approach to opening up dense marsh, usually involving dredges, draglines, bulldozers, and blasting.[123] Various of these methods have been shown to produce abrupt edges less suitable for emergent plants and, therefore, less attractive to swimming waterbirds. Moreover, they rarely achieve the 50:50 cover:water ratio that seems ideal for most waterbirds.[226] I have seen some examples where such methods have produced openings that, after a few years, appear natural;[199] in these cases, blasting[181] or bulldozers were used (as opposed to a dragline) in a fairly dry situation where grading the shoreline was possible either by judicious placement of the charges or by means of the bulldozer scraper blade.[164] Blasting with fertilizer (ammonium nitrate triggered by dynamite) tends to produce "holes" rather than "basins" with gradual edges. Draglines, generally used in very wet situations, also are less easily controlled, especially underwater. An especially drastic method that uses a dragline is level-ditching.[135] Great troughs are scoured through a near-dry marsh bed and the spoil is deposited as flattened ridges between channels. Evaluations of such efforts generally have shown positive results for muskrat and waterfowl populations, and acceptable cost-benefit ratios, but I personally find the product esthetically unsatisfactory. What this system achieves that other efforts lack is a good balance between cover and water, since whole basins, rather than portions, tend to be modified during the operation. If this same interspersion could be achieved with a more natural basin formation, the same benefits should accrue, as well as a more esthetically pleasing outcome, probably at lower cost. However, the technique has proved useful in encouraging the preservation of wetlands for fur production and harvest, and is preferred to the drainage of shallow wetlands less productive of furbearers.

Island building with some of the same tools also has been done, especially for creating nest sites protected from predators; such islands also enhance cover diversity and increase edge. However, naturalness of the island edge is difficult to achieve and, as a result, such islands have been more successful for upland nesting waterfowl, such as the Canada goose and gadwall, than for birds that nest at the marsh edge, like coots and diving ducks.

Artificial methods also may involve short-term programs to modify emergent growth, such as cutting of cattail on ice in winter when water levels are low. When reflooded in spring, plant growth is inhibited and the area may remain open for several years. Although it is costly, this system at least does not produce permanent damage if the design is poor.[222]

Some herbicides have been used successfully to create open areas in marshes, but they are difficult to apply and to control. Moreover, the robust nature of many of the target emergents is such that they may stand for several years before an opening results that attracts birds. Moreover, few of the herbicides are so species-specific that they do not eliminate more favorable species. With several introduced nuisance plants such as water hyacinth, wetlands are impossible to keep open without herbicides; hence, we should not be exploring in the name of conservation the introduction of still other exotic plants that are potential problems.

In addition to the methods applied to manage the marsh itself for wildlife, numerous programs have been designed to provide completely artificial habitat features for nesting birds. These include artificial nest sites for hole-nesting ducks like wood ducks and for platform nesting birds like mallards or Canada geese.[24, 27] They reach their extreme of artificiality in washtubs on posts, or a fiberglass creation with a platform for mallards or Canada geese above and a

Mallard nest on a muskrat house. Nest success in these situations is quite high because of freedom from predators on this muskrat-built "island." Such behavior preadapted the species for use of man-made nesting platforms.

hole for wood ducks below! Most of these devices, though, have gained acceptance by birds, and nest success often is high. Whether we can afford to produce, maintain, and replace a significant number of such structures is one issue; the esthetic element is another.

Fixed or floating platforms have been used to attract loafing or nesting ducks and geese.[201] These structures should be used with discretion, and efforts should be made to have them appear natural.

Such methods and many others advocated may have their place in newly created, artificial, or highly modified situations. Their use as a general operational policy needs to be questioned, or at least more thoroughly evaluated. They are costly in terms of people-power, dollars, equipment, and time, and often leave esthetically displeasing fabrications. Biologically, they can be effective, but they probably do not produce values equivalent to the expenditure.

New Marshes from Old: Marsh Restoration

Fly over the prairies in a wet spring and all low areas —farmed or not—will show the basins of former potholes. As the water seeps through the tiles and ditches, these areas usually, but not always, become dry enough to farm. Some never make good farmland, being always too wet or the soil too peaty for good crops. In such cases, state and federal agencies have tried to reestablish marshes, and fortunately, it seems not too difficult to do.

In those wet years when flooded fields do not drain, marsh emergents often germinate from long buried seeds, surprising everyone.[22] Recent work with soils collected from marshes and with disturbed soil at construction sites in marshes has demonstrated a great variety of seeds present that respond to exposure or to suitable water conditions.[213] Such growths may be rapid and dense, and they create the key physical structure of a marsh, attractive to birds that may respond during the very next nesting season. But obviously, it takes years to duplicate the complex flora and fauna one expects in a long-established, natural marsh. Birds that respond to the life form of the vegetation and the water recognize and test new marshes, but presumably only those where suitable foods have developed can hold a population for long.

Because so many plants and animals of marshes survive because of tolerant seeds or eggs, and because these organisms are distributed by wind, birds, and probably other animals,[12, 49, 130] diversity seems to come quickly to marshes. Much research is needed in this area because more of this type of work will be necessary in the future. Observations on natural succession[46] and processes will allow more accurate predictions of what will happen under various situations.

Marshes Where They Were Not

The creation of entirely new marshes once was only the incidental result of other activity. For example, some functional but not necessarily attractive marshes have been created by the borrow pits of highway or other construction, and by mining for gravel.[35, 85, 208] Coal mining normally results in highly acid water, with reduced plant and animal life, but new methods of handling topsoil have reduced this problem in most areas. However, lakes or ponds or marshes are no longer the end product of coal mining since laws often require a return to premined conditions or to agricultural land, making these areas unsuitable for aquatic wildlife. With proper planning and effort, and little increased cost, such construction digging could produce natural-looking and effective marshes by creating basins of irregular shapes and by modification of steep sidewalls to gradually sloping shorelines.

Recently, mitigation, or legally mandated compensation for damages to wetlands through human activities, has produced many experimental efforts at marsh creation. The loss of wetlands due to highway construction has, in some states, been mitigated by creation of artificial wetlands in contiguous roadside ditches.[25] Such efforts cost thousands of dollars per acre of marsh created but have been tolerated by the economic gains resulting from developments. Such actions are beyond the scope of this book, but wildlifers have had a long history of marsh development efforts that can be applied in these situations. On many wildlife management areas, artificial wetlands have been created for nesting waterfowl, for migratory shorebirds and other waterbirds, and for recreational use. Such areas have proved extremely successful because of the natural invasion of semiaquatic plants and invertebrates that attract wildlife.[46, 211] Direct seeding and planting efforts have been reduced by the discovery that because water-level controls are essential to marsh maintenance anyway, natural seed banks can provide suitable plant communities by use of appropriate water manipulation. Thus, very little direct planting for wildlife management now occurs. However, where mitigation decisions demand rapid replacement of marsh lost to development with newly created marsh, and natural seed banks are not available, transplants, sprouts, and seeding are used in both fresh and saline wetlands.

Birds Versus Fish

It is obvious to the reader by now that a marsh is not a lake, at least most of the time. Even when it is open and lakelike, it often is too shallow to support a major sport fish population. Yet in some areas, such marshes are excellent fishing areas for bullheads, panfish, and occasionally bass, and fishing enthusiasts take a dedicated interest in their condition. But other people are interested in marshes for their potential in aquaculture. Let's examine some of these situations and the conflicts they produce.

First, because lakelike conditions are best for fish, fisherfolk prefer high water levels, usually object to drawdowns (not realizing that these ultimately also benefit fish production), and prefer to eliminate "water weeds"—because they foul motors and fishing tackle. Several guides have been published on improving the fishery values of shallow lakes by weed control[127] that infer improved waterfowl habitat as well.[133] A great variety of herbicides has been used, and underwater cutting bars and grinders are in production and in use. Obviously, all these systems are fighting the natural forces that lead to the plant growth: shallow water and high nutrient availability. Water level increase, which could reduce the aquatic plants, might also make the marsh a lake, thereby destroying much of its potential for waterbirds. But the pressure for fishing areas is great, and the preference for having them in one's "back yard" is nearly as great. Hence, a major policy decision is required. This decision might best be based on the natural history of the area, not the absence of fishing "holes" locally. Those who find the fishing exciting must pursue their quarry with canoe rather than motorboat, and suffer the conflict between hooks and water plants.

Carp-rearing has been in use in Eurasia for centuries and results in major protein production, and the rearing of fish in ponds for commercial purposes is not new even in North America. Putting fish in ponds for recapture has been done for 50 years or more, but the emphasis has been on recovery of hatchery or other special fish stocks for release elsewhere. Recently, the rearing of catfish and other species has flourished in the long growing seasons and warm waters of the southern United States. Now, the use of colder northern ponds has attracted trout raisers who can put the trout in food-rich ponds and retrieve them again before freeze-up.[143] Obviously, the potential for competition between these introduced fish and native fish, amphibians, and birds is very real.[204] Unfortunately, the competition has not been evaluated before such programs are put into operation; this evaluation is essential.

The continuing construction of reservoirs has been responsible for extensive losses of floodplain and riparian wetlands that included considerable marsh, as well as other types of wetland vegetation. These losses have been replaced with wetlands of another sort, shallow lakes, and are tallied in wetland inventories as a net increase in total area.[68a] However, they are of a different class and quality, being better for fish perhaps but less valuable for waterfowl and other waterbirds. They are used by certain ducks and geese as rest and roosting areas on migration and wintering, but they reflect a real net loss in wildlife habitat. Without doubt, some reservoirs have produced excellent marginal marsh, but most are too erratic in water levels to induce the best growth and development of marsh vegetation.

The Coming of the Carp and Other Exotics

The introduction and spread of carp in North America has produced serious and recurring problems in maintenance of marsh quality.[108, 170] I cite it here as an example of human misunderstanding of biological phenomena as well as a problem in management. Carp thrive in places and at densities that no native fish seem to tolerate.[30] As a herbivore or omnivore, it can ingest fine plant foods but can take bottom invertebrates as well. Marshes have proved excellent places for them, and muddy waters, uprooted plants,[207, 210] and food competition result. In northern regions, they may freeze-out from lack of oxygen when heavy snows block sunlight penetration. Only in marshes with water control structures can this species be controlled, and then it presents recurring challenges to management. Poisoning has been resorted to regularly for control, but the cost of poisons and energy costs for application have made this method uneconomical.

All the word on the carp is not in yet, in terms of understanding the species, evaluating its damage, or developing controls, but the carp does demand new approaches if it is to be controlled. Why then are we now releasing another species, the grass carp, widely throughout the south? Although this move is supported by some conservation agencies in the interest of fishing or weed control, other state agencies have strict laws against such introductions. Nevertheless, use of such biological control for reducing the exotic water weed *Hydrilla* has been so successful that such efforts are likely to continue. The unique spawning of this fish in streams makes its natural reproduction in lakes unlikely. If, however, this species gets into marshes, it is likely that it will compete with waterfowl and other fish because it does utilize invertebrates and other water plants also of value to wildlife.[72] Moreover, once the succulent submergent plants have been eaten, grass carp will eat some emergent plants as well.

A number of species of marsh or marsh edge plants have been introduced into new habitats from elsewhere in the world.[53, 71, 166, 191] These include some serious nuisance species such as water hyacinth, Eurasian water milfoil, and Hydrilla, which have cost millions of dollars in control programs here and elsewhere in the world. Salt marsh species, especially Spartina, have replaced native dominants widely around the world. Some of these are results of accidents associated with the movements of man; others were intentional but misguided acts, and will forever influence natural values of our wetlands and mandate management. We must discourage these intentional introductions.

The Limits of Management

As wetlands decrease and user-demand increases, efforts increase to keep productivity of wildlife high. What is the potential of management and what are the limits? Obviously, from the earlier discussion, biologists understand general concepts of plant succession, wildlife habitat selection, and niches of certain groups—but there are many unknowns. Because all environmental influences are not known and are not controllable anyway, management outcomes are not predictable to a high degree of accuracy. We can guess generally what will happen, but surprises are common. Numerous observational studies have been completed, but experimental investigations with tightly regulated controls are nonexistent. Field studies are difficult to control and the usual pattern is to analyze a before-and-after situation. But many of the elements would change in a project of that kind, since years of study must be involved and year-to-year variation is

Marsh management units constructed at the Delta Waterfowl Research Station, Delta, Manitoba, by the Station and Ducks Unlimited, Canada. These units are designed for the experimental study of marsh ecology by permitting replicated experiments of such manipulations as water level, mowing, fertilization, etc.

common. More precise experiments are possible only when experimental units are identical, where experiments can be duplicated concurrently, and when untreated controls can be observed simultaneously. Such units now have been constructed at the Delta Waterfowl Research Station in southern Manitoba with the help of Ducks Unlimited of Canada. These facilities and their findings should create a better understanding of the plant and animal communities that constitute a marsh. Only with such data can precise modeling and prediction become a reality.

All too often we must move from initial research, or even accidental success, to an operational stage in the interest of the resource. This is not good science, but benefits can accrue from these operational programs if managers view themselves as researchers as well. It is rarely possible to repeat any management operation with precisely the same timing, water conditions, and temperature, so each process is unique and requires evaluation. I think the excitement of assessing the outcome of an action program is worth the added time needed to evaluate each and every manipulation. Moreover, such observations will lead to better data, higher accuracy, and more predictable results. Each management operation should be part of a long-term program with preliminary observations, records of the actions taken, and a follow-up measuring successes—regardless of how superficial they may seem.

Management programs require: (1) an assessment of what is desirable and good for wildlife; (2) some observations of natural succession and other wildlife processes, either under different conditions or with several wetland types as examples; (3) some logic in assessing important environmental influences, such as water depth; and (4) some modest experimentation. Armed with these concepts, an amateur can achieve some fair success at managing a duck pond or small marsh area to improve cover diversity and enhance wildlife populations. (See Appendix B.)

But limits on managed systems are also of another sort. In general, we tend to expect too much from technologies and hope that they can save us from sins of the past or present, even replacing major losses of habitat. This is an unrealistic goal for management. We can enhance production, but major increases in productivity due to management usually influence single or a small number of wetlands, not those of large wetland regions.

CHAPTER 9
Marshes and Man

Loss of Marshes—The Good and Bad

As man the builder, farmer, and engineer moved across North America, the marshes and wet prairie soils stood in the way of tillage, railroad and road construction, and other land uses. Drainage was the answer, and millions of acres of land are now underlain with tile, intersected with drainage ditches, and built over, with losses of wetlands reaching millions of acres. Some states lost 95 percent or more of their original marshes. Few could drive across Iowa today and think that it once had 1,196,392 acres of "swamplands" granted to the state for "reclamation."[186] Less than 70,000 acres remain, mostly in state ownership.[23, 131] The United States' total of natural wetlands has been estimated at 127,000,000 acres, of which about 45,000,000 acres or 35 percent were drained by 1950.[186] Perhaps the only plant community that suffered greater loss was prairie. Because of the National Wetland Inventory, some striking figures now are available on recent wetland losses.[68a, 207a] Based on admittedly general early estimates, these suggest that over 50% of all U. S. wetlands have been lost, in spite of some protective legislation, with much of the drainage being for agriculture. Forested wetlands have suffered and are still suffering the most; marshes rank second in losses but often are small areas not easily measured (nor are their wildlife values easily assessed).

Considerable variation occurs in wetland loss by region. Great Lakes marshes have decreased by 71 percent.[95] Southwestern Wisconsin had lost

61 percent of its marshes by 1968; Iowa and Illinois losses probably were close to 95 percent on statewide bases; Michigan was losing 6,500 acres per year in 1978;[6] a small segment of North Dakota lost over 10 percent of the remaining wetland from 1966 to 1980. Minnesota, South Dakota, and North Dakota combined lost an estimated 125,000 acres of prairie pothole wetlands between 1964 and 1968. One estimate is that current losses in the United States are 300,000 acres per year.[10]

Positive benefits of this drainage are the exploitation of some of the richest soils in the world for the food resources and trade products that constitute our high standard of living. Among the detrimental consequences of this drainage were losses of trumpeter swans, cranes, geese, marsh hawks, curlews, and other wetland wildlife. This contrast is reflected in the names of the towns of Plover, Mallard, and Curlew in an area of Northwest Iowa where few marshes remain and the myriads of wildfowl are gone, but where agricultural production is stable and valuable.

Other wetland values lost include water retention, purification, and flood prevention; soil conservation through reduced wind action, erosion control along shorelines; and nutrient concentration. It has been difficult to make an economic case for preserving marshes against the values resulting from other land uses, especially when analyzed on a short-term, cost-benefit basis.[11] Social and political as well as economic influences determine whether drainage occurs. Often, these reasons are personal and short-sighted whereas values of this magnitude should be judged only on a long-term basis, using estimates of net benefits to all users, direct and indirect.

Even more difficult to quantify are losses in population size, species composition, or species richness of birds of areas where extensive drainage has occurred. Losses of the larger birds like swans, geese, and cranes is evident throughout most of the prairie; otherwise, the species composition remains the same but we recognize that the numbers of individuals of each species are much reduced. Some measure of this loss is shown in comparing wet and dry cycles of wetlands with population size of ducks where good annual population estimates are available. Data for mallards and canvasbacks especially demonstrate that populations are highest during and following the wet years, when more wetland breeding sites are available (Fig. 12).[200] Fluctuations of water conditions within a given wetland or wetland complex show similar impacts on population size (Fig. 13). [224] We

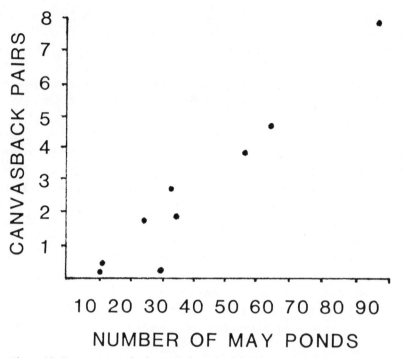

Figure 12. *Data on canvasback populations showing that numbers increase in direct proportion to the numbers of breeding marshes available.*[200]

can use data from such studies to predict what future populations of ducks would be if certain types or percentages of wetlands were permanently drained. In one Northwest Iowa study area, for example, drought dried out all small wetlands just as drainage might do, resulting in an 80 percent decline of blue-winged teal populations.[224] Similar data exist for the effects of drainage on muskrat populations, where declines exceeded 90 percent in an experimental study (See Fig. 5).[225]

Valuating and Evaluating Marshes

Marshes and other wildlife habitats have long been viewed almost entirely for their esthetic values, and biologists have resisted economic analyses even when fighting to preserve areas from destruction. However, economic considerations have the legislative weight and efforts were made first to value components of the marsh, such as a duck or fish, because

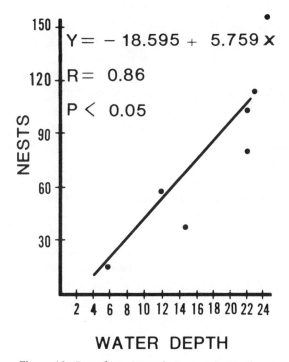

Figure 13. *Data from Dewey's Pasture in Northwest Iowa showing that blue-winged teal populations increased in direct correlation with the increase in water levels on a single pond that was representative of water trends on the entire area.*

it is easier to value a "product" as compared with other more esthetic and recreational aspects. Economists seem to use two approaches to evaluating natural resources like wetlands; either they try to develop novel approaches to placing dollar values on them, or they consider them as entities on which values cannot be placed directly, but on which decisions are made by society. Early assessments involved "pie-in-the-sky" figures, such as $5.00 per duck in the bag or fish in the creel. Some of these assessments seemed valuable and played a role in the preservation of some pricing, giving little support for claims that a valuable resource was being lost.

Another method of assessing certain wildlife recreational value has been to measure expenditures for a sport as hunting. The U.S. Fish and Wildlife Service periodically assesses the values of hunting and fishing to the United States economy and suggests that hunting and fishing are billion-dollar industries.[8] Other economic studies have tried to assess the value of an area to the local economy. Horicon Marsh, in Central Wisconsin, is a large marsh where drainage proved unsuccessful. It was restored by state and federal efforts, and its goose management program was so successful that game harvest and goose watching became major local activities. Hunters bought hunting rights from farmers in the area; even more people came to see the geese and spent considerable money in the area. In 1960-61, it was estimated that communities near Horicon Marsh gained a half-million dollars in sales annually from marsh-associated recreation.[104]

More modern economic valuation involves such things as "willingness-to-pay," a technique that many economists feel can be used to assess the values of esthetic experiences and social values as well as impacts on communities. One such measuring device is a questionnaire that postulates bidding on items or issues; the respondent indicates the limits to which he or she will go to participate in an experience. Another system involves a comparison of travel costs by different users at different distances, with the differential providing an estimate of how increased costs of travel will decrease participation or use.[16] Unfortunately, few of these methods seem to have been used on marsh valuation as distinguished from waterfowl hunting or some other consumptive use. An excellent study of wetland value and duck value in relation to duck populations has achieved a rather sophisticated level of modeling in its estimation of mallard harvest and wetland needs.[81] Studies specific to marshes have included various visual, cultural, and economic valuations,[120, 121] basing economic estimates on the most valuable alternate use of the resource.[80] Some authors have explored the use of assessments that include the areas' potentials for sewage waste treatment and total "life support," such as the production of oxygen, carbon dioxide, carbohydrates, etc.[78] Other economists find these figures unrealistic and encourage the development of comparative figures that are more likely to be accepted.[68]

Public education through the activities of national environmental groups, local nature centers, and state and federal agencies has resulted in much greater appreciation of wetlands values. In a recent study of public attitudes toward wildlife and wildlife habitat, 57 percent of the respondents disagreed with the view that we should fill and build over marshes, as long as endangered species weren't involved.[105] In Florida, almost 72 percent of 250 persons sampled recognized the values of wetlands for wildlife; and 60 percent understood that wetlands control storm surges and floods. Only 20 percent thought they were more of a nuisance than a value. These surveys represent an amazing change in attitudes for an area that has been draining the Everglades for years.

In recent years, societal action through environmental groups and government law-making bodies has resulted in some improvement for preserving wetlands, but more of this has occurred at state and local rather than at federal levels. In many cases, however, the action is to preserve marshes and other wetlands through long-range planning, avoidance, or mitigation for losses. To accomplish this type of preventive action or compensation for damages, evaluations of the marshes must be used as a foundation. The major system now in use to accomplish this evaluation is the Habitat Evaluation Procedure (or "HEP") employed by the U. S. Fish & Wildlife Service. By using various models that assess the suitability of the habitat (formalized as a Habitat Suitability Index) for a certain species or group of species, a per acre "value" is established that is used in mitigation actions where replacement must simulate the total quality and not just the acreage. For example, twice as much land would be required for compensation if its index value was only half that of the land to be lost.

But HEP focuses almost entirely on wildlife values, and the most recent effort to provide rapid, qualitative evaluation systems for wetlands was developed for the Federal Highway Administration.[1] This system takes into consideration the various natural and valuable functions of the wetland as it relates to society, such as water quality enhancement, flood control, primary productivity, as well as food resources and habitats for fish and wildlife, and for passive recreation as well as the more product-oriented fishing and hunting. This system involves a simple quantitative scale so that two marshes can be compared and the unique qualities of a wetland will stand out when compared with any other area; it is being widely tested and improved.

Negative Aspects of Marshes

Although marshes have many, often subtle, values, no one will deny that marshes can create problems for various reasons: excessive water where it isn't wanted; unsuitable soils for farming[11] or construction; and flocks of granivorous birds such as blackbirds or ducks; and, possibly, "weed banks."

Even when tilling and wetlands seem compatible, there are those years when the snow or rain has been heavy, and marsh water levels

An ephemeral pothole (Type I), plowed in the spring but later reflooded. Such mud flats can be favorite places for shorebirds, but reduction of organic matter may reduce its productivity in another season.

Flooded wetland, showing: (a) edges attractive to loafing dabbling ducks, and (b) remains of an old road that formerly ran through the marsh and was abandoned probably because of the maintenance problems of high water and muskrat burrows.

rise to flood out farms, buildings, and roadbanks. Little can be done in such situations, as tiles and ditches are full, pumps have no place to dump the water, and cutting of impediments may do more harm than good. Water-logged soils are no good for construction, and suitable foundations are difficult to build under flood conditions. Road engineers never seem to tire of meeting the challenge, but high water and muskrats usually win out. Many old roadways through marshes have been abandoned, and our slower driving speed may even allow one to examine the marsh while circling it.

The mosquitoes at marsh edges can be a serious nuisance as well as be carriers of disease. However, mosquitoes could thrive without marshes, because of the many species that occur in diverse habitats. Seasonal floodwaters are especially significant as causes of mosquito production. Drainage has not proved to be an effective means of eliminating production sites because many species breed in minimal amounts of water, but some adverse effects on wildlife have resulted from such efforts.[193] Control programs generally are restricted to urban areas where newer, short-lived insecticides are used.

Generally a minor problem in rural areas, marsh odors can be a material issue in urban areas. Because marshes are traps for organic matter, and much decomposition occurs in late summer when water levels decline, rotting vegetation and sulfur-laden gases are not well regarded.

Among the greatest challenges to wildlife managers have been the difficulties inherent in farming adjacent to wetlands, where blackbirds and ducks concentrate. Especially vulnerable crops are wheat and barley in drier prairie regions, corn and sunflowers in the North Central states, corn in the Southeast, domestic white rice in California, Arkansas, Louisiana and Texas, and cultivated wild rice in Minnesota, Wisconsin, and Manitoba. The redwinged blackbird is perhaps the most numerous bird in North America, and breeds in a variety of habitats.[89] They flock in late summer and early fall and feed on ripening corn, sunflowers,[198] and rice[138] in the "milk" and seed stages. If wheat, barley, or oats are swathed to dry, as is still common in areas where it doesn't ripen evenly, blackbirds and ducks both gather to feed. A combination of heavy rain and downed grain is an open invitation for trouble, as much grain is lost from the heads by "puddling" by ducks rather than eating. This depredation is so serious that complete crops have been eliminated in a few days of late July or early August in the southern parts of the Prairie Provinces of

Canada. Various techniques have been used to deter flocks, such as acetylene exploders or gunners to frighten birds away; bait sacrificed to detract birds from more important crops; or chemicals that repel blackbirds from crops (e.g., Methiocarb), but the losses go on and the expenses of farming increase. Because losses often are a matter of timing of ripening, harvest, rainfall, and bird flocking, they usually do not occur every year. Some areas have used crop insurance to minimize the impact on a certain farm in a single season. Nevertheless, the problem is real and, in some areas, may force sociological limits on bird population levels. This is another example of conflict of man and nature where man always expects to win —and doesn't.

Water Level Modification

In some cases, marshes are lost because of misdirected conservation or management efforts. Increased water levels often are cited as desirable goals because the general feeling is that such marshes are more attractive to wildlife. Certainly, they are more attractive to man. High water levels reduce vegetation after several years and, depending on the starting point, tend to create lakes, not marshes, and aquatic rather than semiaquatic communities. I can cite several examples.

Throughout the glaciated Prairie Pothole Region, lakes occur that locally are called marshes, and marshes that are called lakes. Such was the case with Little Wall Lake in Central Iowa. There are many "wall" lakes in the Midwest because they were formed when their drainage was "walled" off by a glacial moraine. But they vary from marsh to lake condition owing to the dynamic water cycles discussed earlier, and their name depended on their condition at the time of survey and naming. This situation may produce local public concern over the lake that looks like a marsh, and many such wetlands have suffered from public pressure to make sure that the body of water looks like what its name is! Such was the fate of Little Wall Lake.

In spite of its sizable acreage (230 to 275 acres), Little Wall Lake was dry in about 1894, 1904, and nearly so in the 1930s and the mid 1950s. But when full, it was a diverse and exciting marsh community, with some sizable water openings. An Iowa Geological Survey report dramatizes both the human conflict, and the character and richness of the "lake":

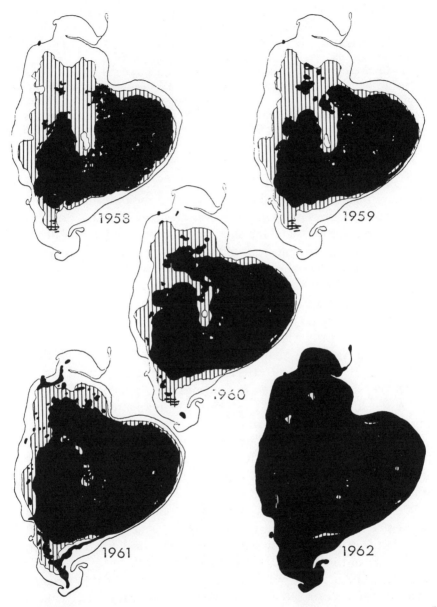

Figure 14. *A water history of Little Wall Lake, showing the open water (black) produced mostly by dredging (1958), dry emergent vegetation (pattern), and sedge or upland edges (white).*[226] *A gradual flooding improved cover water interspersion in 1959 to 1961 and was reflected in increased bird numbers and species richness. Finally, artificially elevated water levels in 1962 eliminated all nesting birds, except for a few red-winged blackbirds and grackles nesting along the perimeter in small trees.*

Had it depth, Little Wall Lake would be the attraction of the landscape, but its shallowness makes it simply a great marsh filled from side to side with aquatic plants. The margins are dark with sedges. In the middle, the cattail lifts its blades undisturbed, while over the deeper waters the pond lilies spread their broad leaves like inverted shields and star the surface with flowers. Innumerable birds fill the air with strident, unmusical sounds; ducks steer their miniature fleets about; mud hens wade among the Calamus roots; blackbirds cry as if life depended upon unceasing verse; the tern hovers above the more open waters or sits upon the sand as if by the sea; the bittern sits among the reeds, bill straight up, more like an inverted stake than any 'stake driver'; and over all, in the evenings, clouds of insects—mosquitoes make gray the air on every side.[128]

The "mosquitoes" were, of course, the midges that swarm on warm and quiet nights in all marshes and they and the birds described still remained (at lower population levels) when Paul L. Errington, authority on muskrats and marshes, first showed me Little Wall Lake in 1957. It was suffering from several years of drought, so that the marsh vegetation was almost dry. But there was a large area of open water, the consequence of dredging the area in 1953. This was an area of about a hundred acres that attracted numerous motor boats.

My observation of the bird life and habitat dynamics of Little Wall Lake spanned nearly eight years,[226] and in its last year was in synchrony with a project that raised the lake level and inundated all vegetation (Fig. 14). The effects of creating a full lake from this former half-marsh caused the loss of most muskrats, mink, and birdlife. A few diving ducks and coots still stop in migration, but it is not a breeding place now. Recreational activities flourished: Fishing was great, as is usual with newly flooded vegetation; a camping area was developed and was constantly filled; and the motor boats, waterskiers, and sailboats created an increased user head-count with significant local economic benefits.

It could have been worse. Many people had recommended drainage, a pattern in this area, which contains some of the deepest and most fertile topsoils in the world. But some local residents favored keeping it, and in 1917, it was proposed that the "wall" be raised to create a dam, that the water level be raised, and that 40 acres be dredged. Fifty years later, it all came to pass. Little Wall Lake became a lake at last.

A few mourned the passing of the marsh, but most people were delighted to see water, if only to park by it momentarily, and viewed the whole project in a positive light. Most viewed this project as a

A large Type III wetland (top) that was drained early in 1979 and planted to forage grasses. This was one of several wetlands drained into a still larger Type IV marsh (bottom), which then was flooded beyond its usual banks.

conservation program and it was financed in part by funds dedicated for that purpose at both state and county levels.

The same effect is felt in areas where small marshes are drained into large ones. Wildlife habitat is lost in both places. Small marshes become farmland, and large marshes become lakes—good for fish but not for waterbirds or muskrats. The effect on wildlife is not as great as when all areas are drained, but the entire character of the area is changed, with a concomitant reduction in wildlife production and species richness.

Water Level Stability

Through a misunderstanding of recommendations directed at preventing drying or flooding of waterfowl nests[90] or muskrat lodges[58] during the breeding cycle, some marsh managers strive for stability of water levels. Observations of nest losses suggest that such stability does induce better nest success and may be a suitable management goal *during* the nesting season but *not* all year. Seasonal and year-to-year variation in water levels are normal events resulting from variation in rainfall. Most marsh organisms are adjusted to these changes. Somehow, we seem to expect maximal wildlife and plant production every year, whereas evolutionary adaptations are a product of optimums or averages; there is security in the flexibility of not being at one extreme or the other. Stability of vegetation is the product of an average of year-to-year conditions. In some years, plants gain in density or coverage; in some years, they lose.

Stable water levels throughout the year have several negative effects. First, nutrients seem to be tied up in organic debris in the substrate, where anaerobic conditions slow decomposition. Reduced emergents result in reduced nutrient pumping into the system, although some submergents also play this role. When the supply of nutrients is reduced, production of other aquatic organisms declines as well. Second, plant communities that require low water levels for either seeding or survival suffer population losses that bring about lake-like conditions. In such cases, marsh life is replaced by lake life.

Marsh managers do not always have the option of regulating water levels, because control structures or water supply do not permit it. In the arid west, where wildlife managers compete for water with other users, water may be available only early in the year. If it is held at high levels for retention into the fall for hunting or other reasons, the effects on vegetation often are disastrous, because seasonal and year-to-year variation is essential for: (1) holding diverse types of vegetation, and (2) making available nutrients for the growth of plants and invertebrates.

Marshes for Water Purification and Energy

There is increasing evidence that water that flows through a marsh comes out cleaner and less enriched with most nutrients than when it entered.[101] Engineers are taking advantage of this cleansing principle, using both natural and cultivated stands of emergent plants, such as cattails, for settling basins and nutrient traps. Some also are experimenting with bogs and salt marshes for purifying human wastes from small communities. These efforts should be regarded as experimental and, it is hoped, will not involve massive operational efforts.[190] Some evidence has been reported that species diversity of plants is reduced by sewage or other pollutants, and that floating plants may be enhanced, as is true in late stages of marsh deterioration when nutrients are more abundant. We certainly don't know and can't predict the long-term effect of such concentrated nutrients on energy flow, species diversity, successional trends, and water quality of a marsh. In agricultural areas, runoff must include significant amounts of pollutants such as fertilizers, which will induce eutrophication of wetlands; herbicides, which will influence plant species composition; and insecticides, which may modify invertebrate populations. These substances need to be monitored in several field situations and studied experimentally to determine the role that marshes play in purifying water.

It is obvious that the marsh is a forgiving and adaptable system; but it should not be viewed as a dump for excess nutrients, any more than it should be used for old cars and other human debris. A variety of aquatic plants can better be used in artificial stands managed specifically for processing human sewage as well as that of livestock and other animal wastes.

Aquatic plants also have been used experimentally for nutrient removal of waste water, with subsequent conversion of this nutrient to plant biomass that can be used for livestock food or for fuel. Some plants, such as duckweed and the introduced submergent *Hydrilla*, produced 13.5 and 15.3 metric tons of biomass per hectare per year in subtropical Florida, which is comparable to temperate terrestrial crops. Water hyacinth had the highest production recorded for any crop, 88.3 metric tons per hectare per year. Based on this production, it has been estimated that a 1000-acre hyacinth farm in the southern United States could produce 10^{12} BTU of energy as methane, and remove nitrogen and other nutrients from waste water for a population of 700,000 people.[177]

Reed, widely used as a building material in Europe and Iraq, has been used in Sweden for burning as a substitute for fossil fuels. With proper selection of cutting area and patterns, reed harvest could be a marsh management tool. Cattail use for energy now is under serious study in Minnesota.[5]

Hence, several possible human uses of hydrophytes have been explored and have potential for the future. Some may adversely affect the marshes; others may not. First and foremost, we must protect the marsh system that creates these plant riches.

Wildlife Users—The Watchers

According to most surveys, wildlife watchers are growing in numbers faster than wildlife users. Obviously, anyone can be a watcher, and current environmental concerns have heightened the public awareness, national programs have enlightened people's attitudes, and nature study centers and television programs have excited youthful minds. Like several European countries, we have become more knowledgeable and more interested in wildlife. The reduced costs of binoculars, telescopes, recorders, and telephoto camera equipment have given many people the chance to be serious students of wildlife, and wetlands often are a focal point for such study. Bird watching is even becoming socially acceptable.

One of the best ways to enhance the appreciation of a wetland is to get people into them. At nature study centers, people are donning hip boots and going into wetlands with plankton nets, magnifying glasses, and cameras. But for the masses, such efforts are unlikely to be undertaken, so alternate systems are used. One of the most helpful is the construction of a walkway through a wetland so that watchers are brought nearer to the sights, sounds, and actions of the animals, by moving through the vegetation. Although doubtless some damage does occur during construction of such ramps, the price is worth the result for a selected few marshes.

Wildlife Users—The Takers

Hunters, trappers, and sometimes fisherfolk are the major users of marsh wildlife. Hunting of waterfowl, rails, and snipe (in some states) is a principal sport and reduced numbers of wetlands have created excessive pressure on remaining areas. The pressure such "users" exerted for the preservation of wetlands preceded any action by wildlife "watchers," and the influence of these users is no less important today. Biologically, such users do little damage to either marshes or their wildlife; their conservation interests do nothing but good.

The philosophy of harvest versus nonharvest is beyond the scope of this review, but the biological issue should be at least presented. Most harvest (hunting, trapping, fishing) utilizes the annual, seasonal surplus of young that normally would be lost to predation, disease, competition, or climatic stress. Such mortality tends to be directly density dependent; that is, mortality is greatest when the population is high, lowest when the population is low. For many species, human harvest replaces other causes of mortality, and does not reduce the population below the normal spring breeding level.[174] However, maximal harvest must be regulated so that populations are protected against disasters such as storms that affect animals regardless of their density.

Because certain species of wildlife are almost entirely associated with wetlands, the major national harvests of such species as ducks and rails can be viewed as products of wetlands. Muskrats, too, have their maximal densities in marshes. A recent summary of such harvest suggests that about 10 million ducks are taken by hunters annually in the United States[37] but no monetary value is generally assigned them as they are not sold. Furbearers, however, constituted a $35 million harvest in 1974-75, with an industry value that would be far greater. Fifty percent of the muskrat harvest occurs in the Midwest, with the largest numbers being in Wisconsin, Minnesota, Ohio, and Iowa. Almost all nutria (97%) were taken in Louisiana, and 58% of the mink were taken in the same states as were muskrats.[37]

Endangered Species and Endangered Habitats

The problems of losses of endangered species have stirred the public interest as have few other wildlife issues. The approaches used to resolve population problems of such species have been unique and often effective. But many endangered or threatened species are rare mainly because their habitat has suffered severe losses. Amazingly few wetland species are among the endangered forms, but several that are have been influenced by losses due to human activities: everglade kites that reside in the Florida Everglades; whooping cranes that nest in the Northwest Territories of Canada and winter in coastal Texas, but which once nested in marshes well south into the Midwest; and the trumpeter swan that is resident in Alaska and British Columbia but also once occurred in midwestern marshes. Several species of rails, especially the Yuma clapper rail in the Southwest, are rare or endangered, but the cause is uncertain. The Houston toad is a small wetland species now considered one of the 10 most endangered species, with only 1,500 animals being crowded out by drainage and housing development.

Obviously, one cannot maintain viable populations of free-living, endangered species without preservation of their optimal habitats. Clearly, the way to keep more species off the endangered species list is to preserve habitats. When habitats become endangered, so will many members of the community, plant or animal. The loss of wetland communities by drainage obviously has reduced the size of many populations of many species of birds, but some have suffered more than others. It is difficult to assess whether whooping cranes and trumpeter swans were ever abundant breeding birds in the Midwest and what caused their disappearance, but both require large ranges for feeding and rearing young. Wetlands in the region now are mostly relicts, often of small size, that are able to hold those adaptable species that have small ranges and diverse food choices. Numerical data are rare and numbers of species haven't changed as much as one might expect, because total loss of habitat hasn't occurred. Our best estimates of losses are shown when wetlands periodically go dry; these results suggest that total loss is possible for many species.

Science

One cannot evaluate the preservation of natural features for scientific study without relating it to human needs. We constantly search for the role of man in nature as well as in human society, and this search for understanding includes the need to know how natural ecological communities function. As scientific approaches, philosophies, and techniques change, we can dig more deeply into such systems or interpret them more fully. It is vital that representative natural systems be preserved for study as well as for their other values. Moreover, these cannot be tiny, isolated, and atypical units; some components of the marsh community (e.g., larger birds) are not attracted to tiny units. In addition, the rarer plants may well be lost unless large, diverse communities are preserved.

Marshes are especially suitable ecological units for observation of natural phenomena by students, and ideal for the scientific study of systems. Because wildlife often concentrates in such energy-rich units, study of these species has unexpectedly enhanced our understanding of sociobiology, mating systems, cyclic phenomena, habitat relationships, population regulation, and other biological facts. Scientists have only scratched the surface: Much research still remains to be done on the dynamics of the plant community in wetlands, in studying nutrient flow, and in developing data bases, allowing us to interpret and predict events in the ever-changing freshwater marsh.

CHAPTER 10
Marshes for the Future

The Human Need for Water

For such a terrestrial creature, man is a perennial seeker of water. Coasts, rivers, and lakes are rimmed with human dwellings, boat landings, overviews, and bathing or wading areas. If water bodies are absent, we build them. Much of this is, of course, for the essential compound of H_2O itself, but there seems also to be an esthetic, visual, and sometimes tactile need for the openness, motion, and reflection of a body of water. In general, the visual clue is essential; just knowing that water is there isn't satisfactory. Thus, a marsh has less "water value" for most people that does a lake. Marshes have not featured as strongly in social or esthetic importance as have other natural features. Except for the Everglades, few wetlands find their way into the National Park System, and have been all but ignored as wilderness areas.[69] Until recently, few would consider building a house overlooking a marsh, whereas lakeshore or riverside property brings the top price.

This attitude does seem to be changing, however. In part because of the wildlife commonly found around marshes, in part because of the quest for open space, urban and rural residents seem now to have greater respect for wetlands and some even seek them out. They add diversity of color, pattern, and form to rather uniform urban areas or fields; they attract a diversity of wildlife that varies with the seasons. The recent outdoor trend has brought canoers in summer and cross-country skiers and snowshoers in winter to marshes where only hunters and trappers passed before. Many still pass the track of mink, weasel, or fox without knowledge or recognition, but we are learning to seek the excitement of the usually unseen. In areas where these wetlands are common, public education has increased, and public awareness and concern for the wetlands and their wildlife are growing.

Wetlands in Conflict

In most areas, our desire for water takes precedence over our wish to understand wetlands or their fauna. Where semiopen marshes occur, we dredge and deepen, or where less water is present, and marshes cannot be filled or drained (for legal reasons, if no other), we build dams to stabilize and deepen the water. This increases property value or makes water areas more attractive to boaters, fishermen, campers, and picnickers. Those who have read to this point now know that such "stability" will result in reduced diversity and production of wildlife and, eventually, even fish. But public pressures and involvements being what they are, many areas often are changed at the hand of man, usually to the detriment of the flora and fauna.

For many years, government policy on wetlands in rural areas was ambivalent: The Soil Conservation Service in the U.S. Department of Agriculture encouraged, engineered, and even subsidized drainage of wetlands in the interest of neater, more efficient, and more productive farming.[122] The U.S. Fish and Wildlife Service, in the U.S. Department of Interior, has encouraged the preservation of wetlands, and leased and purchased them for waterfowl and other wildlife. The Corps of Engineers and Bureau of Land Management developed flood control or land use programs that eliminated wetlands. Such conflict now is less of a problem because of the national policies of these agencies, culminating in 1977 with a Presidential Executive Order to agencies to minimize wetland losses or degradation. The Department of Agriculture has had a special Water Bank Program; stream channelization that seriously affects wetlands[38,56] has been reduced; and the Corps of Engineers now bears responsibility for protection of wetlands from some abuses. However, drainage for agriculture and forestry and certain long-standing water management programs have been excluded from federal regulations.[82] Moreover, less concern is evident in some agencies for smaller wetlands, which are especially vulnerable because they come and go with wet and dry seasons. During the dry years, installation of drainage pipes is easy, and even where marshes are legally protected, illegally installed underground pipes go unnoticed. Unfortunately, a few existing areas of wetland are still threatened by government projects for irrigation or flood control.

Some states and metropolitan areas retain ownership of wetlands and also have laws preventing filling or drainage of most larger wetlands. Many do not, however, and losses continue. In addition, siltation due to poor upland cover management can fill wetlands to a point where they lose their identity,[1] but no legal action is possible. Local interest and attitudes are especially urgent, both because of the potential control states have over wetlands and the support they can give to federal rulings and policies. From 1963 to 1978, 15 states enacted legislation to protect wetlands.[6, 157, 175] Several states have tax incentives to farmers as an inducement to preserve wetlands, whereas in other states, county boards or the governor have prevented the sale of wetlands to federal agencies wishing to preserve in perpetuity.[7, 118b]

Where modifications of wetlands involve a water control structure, excavating, or filling, the U.S. Army Corps of Engineers must provide a permit under Section 404 of the Clean Water Act.[93, 157] The Environmental Protection Agency has veto power over such permits and, from 1975 to early 1980, processed about 12,000 applications for dredge and fill permits in the Midwest region alone.[9] Most were approved because they did not result in complete loss of the wetland; however, any change in wetland water level by fill, impoundment, or water diversion can change it to an entirely different class of wetland with different wildlife, esthetic, and hydrologic functions.

At both national and state levels, the tendency is to delegate control over wetlands to localized boards involved in land-use planning and zoning.[121] This policy may have good and bad aspects, depending on local interests and attitudes. Whatever the level of authority, developers and conservationists are pitted against one another in each move to modify or drain a wetland, and an environmental impact assessment often is required. Each "EIS" tends to be independent of others. In most cases, guidelines are obscure, cause-effect relationships are uncertain, and studies "spawn" reams of paper, while the basic issues are rarely uncovered. Some good comes from such studies, but "paper science" is not the way to discover the values of a wetland or of any other natural resource. We calculate cost-benefit ratios for natural treasures that are priceless and irreplaceable; we compensate for losses by mitigation that may consider only the size of areas, when they are of different types of habitat and serve different purposes. Mitigation laws enforced by the Corps of Engineers, fish and wildlife agencies, and the Environmental Protection Agency often require only that an agreed-upon unit of land be preserved, not that the new wetland be created as a substitute. Hence, a net loss may occur. Moreover, many of the areas created cannot be evaluated later because of personnel shortages, so the mitigation may not result in a functional and permanent replacement. The new concept of "mitigation banking" may have some positive benefits in providing better long-range planning and commitment,[231a] but it also presents some challenges to our evaluation and enhancement techniques. Each case tends to be judged on its own merits, when in fact the cumulative value of one wetland as it is related to others locally or regionally may be the most vital and unappreciated issue.

And who should decide? If raising the level of a marsh floods an adjacent landowner or county, local legal action is possible. If it reduces the wildlife diversity or otherwise influences biological characteristics of the area, what actions can be taken? In legal cases, county action may override city action, or state law dominate county rulings. But rarely does such decision have a sound scientific basis, and each court calls its own set of authorities to meet the questions and challenges, attempting to resolve issues that should involve major policies as well as localized data input. Clearly, this conflict is not easily resolved, but it can be eased by developing a national policy that would incorporate the best elements of resource conservation for the good of the nation.

Conservation Goals and Policies

One of the greatest causes of conflict in conservation programs is identifying, establishing, and communicating the objectives of the program. Thus, establishing sound practices within the responsible agency (governmental or private) is difficult, and the public is confused and concerned about the techniques used to achieve these goals.

Decision-making on wetland preservation, as on that of other land uses, is in need of serious revision. Additional socio-economic and biological data will enable further quantitative assessments, modeling, and predictions and thus a better basis for decisions. But not all policy need be quantitatively, and especially economically, based. I see no reason why governmental agencies shouldn't have policies that reflect esthetic, philosophic, and other noneconomic or nonpolitical considerations. Moreover, such organizations should exercise leadership, making use of the wisdom, motivation, and excitement of the experts they employ. National concerns, public expressions, and pressures will influence the evolution of any policy, but the mood of the masses is vital to the conservation of wetlands—as it is in all conservation.

Local, state, and federal perspectives must be coordinated into an integrated policy that will serve humankind now and in the future. There is some national leadership today and much national interest in conservation,[118b] but it will take many years to achieve a functional national policy. The Water Bank Program of the Department of Agriculture; the revised responsibilities of the Corps of Engineers in protecting wetlands;[228] the regional centers for the study of wetlands such as those in Georgia, Florida, and Louisiana; the private, legal, and technical gatherings of interested persons in private wetland organizations[76, 79] are but a few of the expressions of national interest in this area.

Our future land ethic must give priority to our natural resources. Human intelligence, the prime achievement of the evolutionary process, is nevertheless the main force that can destroy our natural heritage and natural systems; and it is the only power that can preserve them. This power, it seems to me, gives us a moral obligation to preserve natural communities such as marshes. Obviously, current attitudes toward preserving endangered species reflect general agreement with this philosophy. But what are the limits of our dedication? Are they a matter of convenience or economics, and do they change with human attitudes and goals generation by generation? Predictions of human population growth and impacts make it obvious that natural resources will continue to dwindle at alarming rates.[15] Despite the appreciation of resource values by present and future generations, we will lose these and other natural components of our national heritage if population pressures continue to grow.

Epilogue

You, the reader, must now face a decision vital to the future of wetlands and their wildlife in North America. I hope that understanding
and concern have been enhanced by this reading, and that action is
the next step. This action may take many forms: For some, it may
be the investment of time or money in private acquisition programs,
such as those of The Nature Conservancy or the National Audubon
Society. For others, it may be political action at local, state, or
national levels. Still others may express and defend an opinion over
the dinner table, an action even more effective if overheard by our
children. But all these acts, subtle to dramatic, must one day lead us
to a national policy that will bring about the retention, management,
and widespread use of one of our most unappreciated natural resources—freshwater marshes.

APPENDIX A
Some Elementary Marsh Study Techniques

Although numerous textbooks and laboratory manuals describe techniques for the study of freshwater organisms,[219] plant communities, and animal populations,[74] or show how to cover-map habitat, few of these books emphasize marshes. Examples of a few such techniques may reduce the fear of some experimentation and observation by nonprofessionals. In addition, there is no better way to learn about marshes than to get into them. The techniques outlined here provide an excuse to go into a marsh and examine in some detail what is there. Little damage is done in examining a marsh system, and much can be gained by students of any age or profession. Moreover, familiarity with such techniques aids in interpretation of environmental impact statements and other documents to which the lay public is now exposed.

Your First Step—in the Marsh

First, one needs to conquer the fear of a marsh as a bog or quicksand, where a pole or man will sink for 20 feet. Marshes do sometimes have muck bottoms and are soft and sticky. Marsh walking often *is* hard work, but even though you may fall in a time or two before developing "marsh legs," I've never seen anyone disappear in a marsh. Moreover, some marshes are very solid, being either sand or solid root stalks. A canoe paddle or walking stick is a helpful aid.

Second, wear rubber hip boots or chest waders, or at least protective shoes and pants. Old plant stalks can be sharp and painful, and bottles and other debris in marshes can be dangerous. Moreover, even experienced marsh professionals dislike the leeches that are abundant at some marsh phases, or the "swimmer's itch" that can be caused by a harmless but irritating larval parasite of waterbirds.

In southerly areas, one must be wary of snakes, although they are more likely to be associated with riverbanks or swamps.

Canoeing or boating in a marsh is hard work, but may be necessary when three feet of water and some mud make walking difficult or impossible for amateurs. Poling a canoe or boat is a technique soon perfected by those who must push through dense vegetation. In the Everglades, and now in larger marshes of the north, airboats are used by professionals or hunters who must travel long distances in marsh vegetation where motor boats will not function.

An easy way to gain experience in a northern marsh is to examine it during the winter after freeze-up. Wearing slip-resistant boots, snowshoes, or skis, one can "walk on water," gaining a most valuable perspective. Moreover, there are surprises in the activities of mink, weasels, muskrats, deer, and winter birds.

Some Scientific Philosophy

Regardless of your reasons for gathering data about a marsh, learn to do it quantitatively. It is best to use an accepted, published standard, as may be found in one of several technique manuals, but when developing a new technique, use it throughout a series of observations or experiments. If you are comparing the number of snails in two habitats, use a sampling net of the same area and mesh size, and the same number of dips or sweeps in all sampling sites so that you have comparative data. Counting blackbirds, muskrat houses, or anything similar should follow a standardized system.

It is also advantageous to separate observational versus experimental procedures. One can make observations, even quantitative ones, but not know whether these are typical, unless repeated observations are made. It is even more difficult to assess the causes (as opposed to effects or occurrence) of biological events without being able to experimentally produce them and even duplicate the experiment. Hence, experimental studies, obviously the most difficult and costly, are also most likely to yield undeniable results and to facilitate identification of causes of observed effects. Although you may not wish to involve yourself in such sophisticated studies, this scientific logic helps you to evaluate the work of others, and avoid accepting statements when they lack supporting quantitative and experimental data.

Plant Presence, Cover, and Density

Many methods of plant assessment can be followed, but the selection of a technique depends on whether one is simply assessing presence or absence of a species, or whether quantitative data are needed on the distribution and population size. Although it is difficult to obtain agreement about techniques, standardization in a single series of observations will help resolve many of the difficulties typically encountered in plant survey.

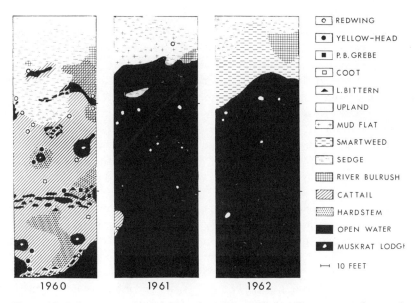

Figure 15. *Belt transect through the edge of a marsh that forms a general map of vegetation and open water on which muskrat lodges and bird nests are plotted.*[226]

Cover mapping can be done to provide patterns of distribution of emergents by species. Such cover mapping is difficult if the water is deep, and in northern areas, I've found it easiest to do on ice in winter. Although some changes occur with new vegetation, this is the vegetation that greets birds on their arrival and that influences where their activities will take place. Such mapping can also be done from aerial photos if they are available in local offices of the Soil Conservation Service or associated agencies. Randomly selected belt transects or quadrats can be used when marshes are too large for total assessment (Fig. 15).[226]

Detailed vegetation data usually are obtained by one or several of the following methods: *Point-count transect.* The easiest system is to stretch a tape over a randomly selected area and record plants found at each one-foot or one-meter interval (for example);[225] the spokes of a wheel, a frame set up at intervals with spear-points that touch vegetation, etc., also can be used. The major concept is the randomness of the chance to encounter various plants, so that the abundant ones should be recorded most often and in proportion to less abundant species. This system also can be used to show the distribution of open water, water depth, and types and location of submergent plants.

The *Line-intercept* method is similar, but all plants touching or near one side of a tape are tallied. Numbers, therefore, are larger and distribution also is shown. Often this method is combined with point-counts at set intervals, to quantify records of water depth, submergents or open water.

Small quadrats are especially favored where detailed plant observations are to be made. One can set these out randomly by gridding an area, numbering the intersections or plots, and using a table of random numbers for selection. Or numerous less-structured systems can be found. For statistical measurement of variation, three samples are minimal, but this small sampling is unlikely to achieve a significant level of population assessment. The number of plots needed usually may be assessed grossly by finding the number at which measured changes are no longer significant. If, for example, you do 12 quadrats, and the number of species found and their distribution doesn't change from numbers 8 through 12, chances are good that a sample size of 8 or 10 will accurately record what you want. Obviously, this sample size varies with the number of species present, their spatial distribution, and their numerical abundance.

Quadrats of rectangular shape seem to be preferred by many plant ecologists. Data recorded in the quadrat can vary from clipping and counting to detailed cover-mapping. In some cases, "exclosures" are used to keep herbivores out of the plots, allowing the assessment of the amount of cover consumed by muskrats or birds. "Relative abundance" data may be gained on cover (areal distribution of plants), by ranking in percent or numbers; detailed information on procedures should be obtained from a current plant ecology text.

A final note about plants. Plant life-form, rather than details of species, may be all that is necessary for some studies. In such cases, the mapping of tall versus short emergents, or distribution of submergents versus emergents may be a less demanding task than those outlined above. However, the procedures are the same.

Water Characteristics

Limnological methods tend to be rather complex for amateurs but some excellent texts are available that provide a good background for comprehension of the patterns and processes that occur in water.[229] Chemical analysis of dissolved solids in the water is of particular interest, because there tends to be a correlation between high concentrations and high biological productivity. These concentrations are usually measured electrically by specific conductance and require a fairly expensive instrument. However, some features of the water can be measured simply, such as water clarity and pH. Water turbidity is of special interest in marshes because they tend to be clear, and intrusions of silt or of nutrients that cause algal blooms are conspicuous. An easily made, patterned disk tied to a measuring rope can be lowered into the water until the pattern is obscured. The measured depth is an index to clarity, and microscopic examination may reveal the cause of turbidity. Although the hydrogen ion concentration (pH) may not be useful information except where it is extreme, it is easily measured with pH paper available from biological supply houses. Most inland, freshwater marshes range from near normal (6.5 - 7.0) to alkaline (8.0 - 8.5). Highly acid bogs may be 4.5 - 5.5.

Invertebrate Richness and Abundance

The diversity and abundance of the larger (macroscopic) insects, snails, crustaceans, and other less well-known groups of invertebrates discourage amateur study. But the more common forms can be sorted and easily placed in large taxonomic categories,[147, 161] providing the opportunity to see the diversity and abundance of life often found in seemingly sterile waters.

Swimming invertebrates usually are sampled by nets or traps. For very small planktonic forms, fine-meshed sweep nets or drag-nets are preferred. They can be simulated by cheesecloth, plastic mesh, or fine metal screen, but still finer nets of durable quality must be purchased at special biological supply houses. Dip nets with modest-sized openings (20 meshes per inch) let water and silt pass through, while trapping the larger, more visible invertebrates of greatest interest to the amateur. Minnow traps, available in sporting goods stores, also work for dragonflies and other aquatic nymphs, and for swimming adults. Dragonflies, damselflies, midges, caddis flies, mosquitoes, and so forth, that leave the water as flying adults, can be quantified in small cages or emergence traps built over the water, which hold those insects that have emerged in that surface area.

Many of the larger invertebrates of marshes are bottom or benthic forms that can be sampled by various dredges and corers.[159] Some precise and expensive samplers designed specifically for bottom sampling work well in mud, sand, or even gravel bottom[106] but are useless in marshes because of the plant debris and root stalks. Corers can be made of plastic drain pipe or tubing such as that used in plumbing. When the edge is sharpened, they can be forced into the substrate by rotating as they are pushed. If plugged with a cork or the standard screw top, the suction holds the debris in the tube as it is quickly transferred to a bucket. Such dredge materials then must be washed through sampling screens and the remains sorted. This can be an exciting process, revealing the variety and abundance of invertebrate life.

Flying insects can be taken by "butterfly" net, or by "sticky-trap"—an adhesive sprayed on boards of specific sizes where landing insects are caught.

Birds

Much of the interest in animals of marshes centers on birds because of their variety, density, colors, and conspicuous behavior. Armed with binoculars and a bird guide, the amateur can easily assess species richness, relative abundance, distribution by vegetative type, and so on. Because of legal protection, the difficulty of finding nests, and concern for disturbance of nesting birds, the census of birds often is best directed to counts of singing males on perches (blackbirds, sparrows, wrens), loafing sites (ducks, geese), or feeding pools (grebes, coots). However, some species are best counted by their nests because the adults are so inconspicuous (bitterns and grebes), or occur in such large colonies of densely packed nests (egrets, herons, ibises), that they cannot be estimated properly from a distance. Where whole marshes or cover types cannot be censused, blocks or quadrats (Figure 15), strip transects, or even line transects can be used as sampling units to compare two areas or habitats.

Mammals

Marsh-dwelling mammals are extremely difficult to census, and trapping is complicated by legal problems and permits, by techniques, and by difficulties of data interpretation that prevent the beginner from doing meaningful work. Records of trappers' catches of mink, weasels, and muskrats are extremely useful population measures, but are of unknown quality. Indexes to mammal use, such as numbers of muskrat lodges or the incidence of mouse or muskrat clippings, provide some crude measure when variation in populations is extreme. In large areas these are best sampled via intercepting transects or quadrats.

Amphibians and Reptiles

Although qualitative sampling for species identification, age, or stage of development can be done by hand-grab, by dip net, and even by mammal snap-traps on the shoreline, quantitative data are difficult, if not impossible, to obtain. Some ingenuity is needed to resolve this problem.

Fish

Even though game species are rarely involved, restrictions may be placed on fish sampling by conservation agencies. Laws differ from state to state and should be checked first. Netting is the usual means of capturing fish in ponds or lakes, but nets are fouled by algae or vegetation and are difficult to place in marshes. Dip nets occasionally catch fish, but provide no systematic approach or quantitative data. Minnow traps work for some species but not for others. Selective poisons and electric shocking have been used by professionals, but they may be dangerous and require special permits. Moreover, the data are difficult even for professionals to evaluate.

APPENDIX B

Managing Duck Hunting or Furbearer Areas

Sportmen who own or lease marshes specifically for the harvest of waterfowl, rails, or snipe — or land owners wishing to manage and lease suitable wetlands for hunting or trapping — should find the general management procedures described earlier to be satisfactory for managing foods attractive to waterfowl and cover useful for hunting. However, whereas nesting ducks are tied to emergent cover for nest sites or brood cover, and to small pools that provide territorial isolation, birds in fall migration or during winter travel in flocks and go where the food is.

Waterfowl management areas include marshes and several other kinds of palustrine wetlands such as shrub or forested swamps. Many of these wetland types contain some marsh vegetation important to waterbirds, mammals, and other vertebrates for food, and provide protection from weather and predators. The most common categories of wetland management areas are: 1) *moist-soil impoundments*, emphasizing the development of shallow marsh plants productive of seeds used by waterfowl in the nonbreeding period;[68b] 2) *emergent marshes*, favoring more permanent perennial plants used for food by muskrats, nutria, and for hunter cover; and 3) bottomland floodplain areas called *"greentree reservoirs,"*[178a] where food resources such as acorns and other tree mast are utilized.

Emergent vegetation is used mainly for protective cover in strong winds, although some duck species still feed there. However, after the breeding period of adults and the major growth period of young of the year, ducks switch from insect and crustacean foods to vegetative materials. These include: (a) seeds such as those of wet-meadow smartweeds or millets, deeper water sago pondweed, or upland agricultural grains for some dabbling ducks;[26] (b) leafy vegetation such as sago pondweed in central marsh pools or shallow lakes; and (c) tubers such as those of sago pondweed prized by canvasbacks, or duck potato used by various dabbling ducks. Certainly, they still eat animal foods and some ducks that winter in coastal estuaries and bays even take a variety of marine foods. However, ducks are less dependent on animal foods in winter and management can be directed toward shallow water and natural crops of wet-meadow species. Before marsh ecologists recognized the abundant supply of residual seeds in the substrate, it was common for them to collect or grow seeds for planting, or dig tubers or plants for hand planting.[54, 83, 118] Under most conditions, supplemental seeding is not essential and adds greatly to management costs. Nor are special foods necessary to attract ducks and geese; natural foods are, in fact, best.

Water-level control is essential for any management program. Where natural outlets occur, a small impoundment and simple water control structure often can be added[13] with little permanent disturbance or visibility. I have seen effective management with hand-made earthen dikes removed or replaced only as needed. Simplicity is the key to cost effectiveness. At most, a small duck marsh needs only a simple concrete-supported stop log of $2'' \times 4''$ boards to allow regulation to 2-inch depths.[185] Various manuals containing guidelines are available, and examples can be seen at many wildlife management areas. State and federal regulations must be checked with both fish and wildlife and water management agencies to determine limitations and to acquire any necessary permits.[64a]

Some experimentation is necessary on each area to understand soil characteristics, seed stocks, patterns of water availability, and chronology of migration as it influences waterfowl use. The general management strategy is to reduce water levels in mid to late summer to induce germination of natural wet-meadow plants such as smartweed, millets, and tuber-producing sedges. Once the annuals have seeded, they are reflooded to facilitate access by dabbling ducks to these plant foods and, probably, to invertebrate populations that have developed there. In most cases, survival of these plants until the next year is not essential but, as seen earlier, perennial plants also may seed at this time. Reflooding in spring may help kill unwanted plants such as seedling willow and cottonwood trees or cattail, but controlling these plants could require more rigorous control methods.[148, 149]

As simple as this procedure might appear, some limitations are enforced by plant foods and the species of ducks using the area. Growth of sago pondweeds and other submergent plants may be harmed by drawdowns that produce good crops of seeds on wet-meadow species, so foods for dabbling ducks are favored over those that attract diving ducks. Most marsh water control structures do not permit total drawdown, and the deeper central portion of the marsh may retain enough water for such submergents to survive. With full water-level control, careful management of water levels can be used to allow both a wet-meadow zone around the perimeter and survival of submergents in the central area.

Small marshes often can pay for themselves in harvest of furbearers (as well as use or leasing for waterfowl hunting), especially when fur prices are high. However, management procedures for muskrats must be balanced with management programs for waterfowl harvest or production. Complete drying of marsh areas as in a late summer drawdown induces losses of muskrats that move to wetter areas or suffer increased natural predation. Reproduction probably is inhibited, so overall annual production is reduced. Thus, the level of a single marsh should not be lowered to a level at which muskrat populations are eliminated. Reducing populations, however, may prevent eat-outs and sustain harvest over a longer period, and often benefits duck harvest by maintaining good interspersion of cover and water. Certainly, excellent hunting may occur in wide open areas (especially for diving ducks), but diverse patterns of cover water and foods provides a diversity of wildlife use and potential harvest.

In some places, conservation-minded hunters managing marshes in natural breeding areas may want to create suitable conditions for breeding waterbirds as well as for hunting; water levels in these areas should not be lowered during the nesting period, and preferably not in the brood-rearing period unless there are alternate feeding locations. In most areas, late summer drawdowns still produce enough seeds and other foods attractive to migrant waterfowl, rails, and snipe. Where water levels are influenced solely by natural fluctuations, the management of muskrats or nutria can be used to make some beneficial changes in open water-emergent cover patterns and ratios. Some managers tend, however, to reduce trapping to encourage buildup of herbivores that open emergents by cutting for lodges and food. But because eat-outs by muskrats are common and are difficult to correct in the absence of water control for drawdowns, intensive and continuous control of muskrats is the best policy. The natural productivity of muskrats and the difficulty of controlling them usually create periodic "highs" that reduce emergent populations. Where population highs threaten an area, and trapping is impossible or ineffective, summer drawdowns can be used to limit breeding populations and winter drawdowns to reduce habitability of the area and force rats to move out. Again, timing must be regulated in relation to nesting ducks or other waterbirds. Where muskrats, nutria, or livestock do not create openings in dense marsh vegetation, the area may be less attractive to birds. Water level management is the best alternative where available, but some more artificial methods may be necessary such as cutting, digging, or blasting.

APPENDIX C
Scientific Names of Plants and Animals Mentioned in the Text

Alligator *Alligator mississippiensis*

Arrowhead *Sagittaria* spp.

Backswimmers (Notonectidae)

Bass, Largemouth *Micropterus salmoides*

Beaver *Castor canadensis*

Beetle, Predaceous Diving (Dytiscidae)

Beetle, Whirlygig (Gyrinidae)

Beggarstick *Bidens* spp.

Bison *Bison bison*

Bittern, American *Botaurus lentiginosus*

Bittern, Least *Ixobrychus exilis*

Blackbird, Redwinged *Agelaius phoeniceus*

Blackbird, Yellow-headed *X. xanthocephalus*

Bladderwort *Utricularia* spp.

Bobolink *Dolichonyx oryzivorus*

Bug, Giant Water (Belostomidae)

Bullfrog *Rana catesbeiana*

Bullhead, Black *Ictalurus melas*

Bulrush, Alkali *Scirpus paludosus*

Bulrush, Hardstem or Tule *S. acutus*

Bulrush, River *S. fluviatilis*

Bulrush, Softstem *S. validus*

Burreed *Sparganium* spp.

Cactus, Prickly Pear *Opuntia* spp.

Caddis flies (Tricoptera)

Canvasback *Aythya valisineria*

Carp *Cyprinus carpio*

Carp, Grass *Ctenopharyngodon idella*

Cattail *Typha* spp.

Celery, Wild *Vallisneria americana*

Chufa or Flatsedge *Cyperus esculentus*

Clam, Fingernail *Sphaerium* spp.

Coot, American *Fulica americana*

Copepod, e.g. *Cyclops* spp. (Copepoda)

Cottonwood *Populus deltoides*

Crane, Whooping *Grus americana*

Crane flies (Tipulidae)

Crayfish (Decapoda)

Curlew, Long-billed *Numenius americana*

Cutgrass, Rice *Leersia oryzoides*

Cyclops (Copepoda)

Damselflies (Odonata)

Daphnia or Water Fleas (Cladocera)

Dove, Mourning *Zenaidura macroura*

Dragonflies (Odonata)

Duck, Fulvous Whistling *Dendrocygna bicolor*

Duck, Ruddy *Oxyura jamaicensis*

Duck, Sea (Tribe Merginini)

Duck, Inland Diving *Aythya* spp.

Duck, Wood *Aix sponsa*

Duckweed, Common *Lemna minor*

Duckweed, Star *L. trisulca*

Egret, Cattle *Bubulcus ibis*

Eider *Somateria* spp.

Flatsedge or Chufa *Cyperus esculentus*

Fox, Red *Vulpes fulva*

Gadwall *Anas strepera*

Gallinule, Common *Gallinula chloropus*

Goose, Canada *Branta canadensis*

Goose, Snow *Anser caerulescens*

Grebe, Eared *Podiceps nigricollis*

Grebe, Horned *P. auritus*

Grebe, Pied-billed *Podilymbus podiceps*

Grebe, Red-necked *Podiceps grisegena*

Grebe, Western *Aechmophorus occidentalis*

Gull, Franklin's *Larus pipixcan*

Hawk, Marsh *Circus cyaneus*

Heron, Black-crowned Night *N. nycticorax*

Heron, Great Blue *Ardea herodius*

Heron, Little Blue *Florida caerulea*

Heron, Tricolored *Hydranassa tricolor*

Hyacinth, Water *Eichornia crassipes*

Hydrilla *Hydrilla verticillata*

Ibis, White-faced *Plegadis chihi*

Jellyfish, Freshwater *Craspedacusta sowerbyi*

Jewelweed *Impatiens* sp.

Juncus or Rush *Juncus* spp.

Killdeer *Charadrius vociferus*

Leech (Hirudinea)

Loon, Common *Gavia immer*

Mallard *Anas platyrhynchos*

Mayflies (Ephemeroptera)

Meadowlark *Sturnella neglecta*

Midge or Marshflies (Chironomidae)

Millet or Barnyardgrass *Echinochloa* spp.

Mink *Mustela vision*

Moose *Alces americana*

Mosquito (Culicidae)

Mouse, Meadow *Microtus pennsylvanicus*

Muskrat *Ondatra zibethicus*

Muskrat, Round-tailed *Neofiber alleni*

Nutria *Myocastor coypus*

Oriole, Northern *Icterus galbula*

Ostracods or Seed Shrimp, e.g. *Candona* spp. (Ostracoda)

Otter *Lutra canadensis*

Owl, Snowy *Nyctea scandiaca*

Pheasant, Ring-necked *Phasianus colchicus*

Pike, Northern *Esox niger*

Pondweed *Potamogeton* spp.

Pondweed, Sago *P. pectinatus*

Potato, Duck *Sagittaria* spp.

Ptarmigan, Willow *Lagopus lagopus*

Raccoon *Procyon lotor*

Rail, King *Rallus elegans*

Rail, Sora *Porzana carolina*

Rail, Virgina *Rallus limicola*

Rail, Yuma Clapper *Rallus longirostris yumanensis*

Rat, Rice *Oryzomys palustris*

Redhead *Aythya americana*

Reed, Common *Phragmites communis*

Rush *Juncus* spp.

Salamander, Tiger *Ambystoma tigrinum*

Sandpiper, Upland *Bartramia longicauda*

Scuds or Sideswimmers (Amphipoda)

Sedge *Carex* spp.
Shoveler *Anas clypeata*
Shrew, Short-tailed *Blarina brevicauda*
Shrimp, Fairy *Branchinecta* spp.
Shrimp, Seed (Ostracoda)
Sideswimmers or Scuds (Amphipoda)
Smartweeds *Polygonum* spp.
Snake, Garter *Thamnophis* spp.
Sowbugs (Isopoda)
Sparrow, Song *Melospiza melodia*
Sparrow, Swamp *Melospiza georgiana*
Sponge, Freshwater (Spongillidae)
Strider, Water (Gerridae)
Stork, Wood *Mycteria americana*
Swallow (Hirundinidae)
Swan, Trumpeter *Cygnus buccinator*
Teal, Blue-winged *Anas discors*
Tern, Black *Chlidonias niger*
Tern, Forster's *Sterna forsteri*
Toad, Houston *Bufo houstonensis*
Turtle, Blanding's *Emydoidea blan-dingii*

Turtle, Mud *Kinosternon* spp.
Turtle, Painted *Chrysemys picta*
Turtle, Snapping *Chelydra serpentina*
Water-crowfoot *Ranunculus* spp.
Water Fleas, e.g. Daphnia spp. (Cladocera)
Water Lily, Yellow *Nuphar advena*
Water Milfoil *Myriophyllum* spp.
Watermeal *Wolfia* spp.
Water Rat or Round-tailed Muskrat *Neofiber alleni*
Weasel, Least *Mustela rixosa*
Weasel, Short-tailed *Mustela erminea*
Whitetop *Scolochloa festucacea*
Wigeon Grass *Ruppia* spp.
Willow *Salix* spp.
Wren, Marsh or Long-billed Marsh *Cistothorus palustris*
Wren, Sedge or Short-billed Marsh *Cistothorus platensis*
Yellowthroat *Geothlypis trichas*

Appendix D

Glossary of Terms Used in the Text

Adaptation. Genetically based modifications in anatomy, physiology, and behavior that better equip an organism to deal with its environment.

Alkali lakes. Bodies of water located in areas where a high rate of evaporation concentrates salts such as sulfates and chlorides.

Basin. Topography of the land that creates a depression that holds water.

Benthos. Organisms like clams that use the bottom of the marsh or lake, and which sometimes are imbedded in the substrate soil and organic matter.

Biomass. The total weight of living material (plant and animal) found on a site or sample area.

Capillary action. A physical action produced by surface tension that draws water upward through fine pores in the soil in opposition to gravitational forces.

Competition. The negative interaction of two organisms seeking to use the same resource, such as food or habitat.

Cover-water ratio. The percentage of cover in relation to the total of open water; e.g., 50:50 equals half of each.

Decomposition. The combined processes by which organic matter is broken down from its original form to its organic and inorganic constituents by leaching, detritivores, bacteria, and fungal decomposers. Some ecologists restrict the use of this term to action by decomposer organisms.

Detritivore. Organisms that utilize dead organic tissue like that of plants as food, and break it into smaller and smaller pieces.

Diversity. Infers the variety of life, usually viewed positively by wildlife managers.

Drawdown. The (usually) intentional lowering of water levels for the purpose of allowing germination of seeds in the substrate. Sometimes used to describe conditions resulting from a drought.

Ecology. The science that studies organisms in relation to their environment and attempts to explain patterns and processes that make biological systems work.

Ecosystem. A community of living organisms and their physical environment that function as an entity in energy flow and nutrient cycling.

Ecotone. A term once used commonly to describe the edge between major plant communities, e.g., grassland and forest. Some employ the term to describe any vegetational edge.

Emergent. A plant that grows rooted in shallow water but the bulk of which emerges from the water and stands vertically. Usually applied to herbaceous rather than woody vegetation.

125

Endangered species. A species of animal or plant so rare that is put on a special list by the U. S. Fish & Wildlife Service.

Environmental impact statement. A document prepared to outline and justify an action such as construction that will modify the environment substantially. Often includes preventive or compensatory action.

Eutrophication. The process of gradual enrichment that occurs in a body of water through natural inflow and accumulation of nutrients, or indirectly through human action such as fertilization in upland grass or crops.

Evaluation. The qualitative or quantitative process of assessing the value of a habitat for wildlife. Currently done by most federal agencies using the Fish & Wildlife Service's Habitat Evaluation Procedure (HEP).

Everglades. A unique wetland type in southern Florida made up of communities of interspersed tropical trees and grasses not found elsewhere in the U. S.

Exotic. An organism from a foreign country released intentionally or accidentally in this country and that survives here. Often very successful as a species but may compete with native forms.

Fen. A unique and localized sedge-moss wetland produced where slightly alkaline water emerges at the surface. Bogs have similar types of vegetation but tend to be acid.

Furbearers. Diverse mammals, such as muskrats and mink, that are trapped for their pelts, which have commercial value.

Germination. The process of embryo development and growth of a seedling plant from a seed, usually induced by a specific set of moisture, temperature, and chemical conditions.

Glacial. Refers to any product or action of glaciers such as the sheet glaciers that once covered northern North America and that created myriads of marshes in the prairie region of the U. S. and Canada.

Great Basin. An intermountain region of the western United States characterized by low rainfall, high evaporation, and highly saline lakes. Water supplies to such marshes often originate from snowmelt in the mountains.

Habitat. The place where an animal (or plant) resides and finds food, water, cover, and space.

Habitat diversity. A qualitative statement of the structure of the vegetation that forms potential habitats for wildlife. Generally speaking, the more diverse the structure, the more potential habitats exist for diverse wildlife. Usually one of the objectives of wildlife management.

Hydrology. The study of water movement on the earth's surface and in the underlying soil and rocks.

Hydroperiod. The duration of flooding or water presence in a wetland. This usually dictates what plants germinate and grow.

Insolation. Absorption of sunlight by the earth or by the water's surface.

Instability. Variation in physical factors such as water depth that influence and even regulate biological processes such as plant growth.

Irrigation. A system devised to capture and distribute water in suitable amounts and timing for agricultural crops.

Limnology. The science that deals with the biological, chemical, and physical properties of water.

Management. As opposed to businesses where this term refers to the personnel in charge of the operation, wildlife managers use the term to infer the strategy and techniques that will be used to achieve specific goals.

Marsh. A community of water-tolerant, soft-bodied emergent plants (and associated animals) usually found in a basin of shallow water or on saturated soils fed by underground water sources.

Mitigation. Avoidance of or compensation for damages to natural habitats resulting from human developments.

Niche. The role that an organism plays in an ecosystem. For example, a plant is a primary producer, and an animal is one of three types of consumer: "carnivore" (animal eater like a mink), "herbivore" (plant eater like a muskrat), or "omnivore" (plant and animal eater like a human being).

Nutrient. A chemical substance of value as a food component for plants and animals. Nutrients are incorporated by plants and then eaten by animals. Recycling of nutrients through the ecosystem is dependent upon detritivores and decomposers.

Oligotrophic. As opposed to an enriched (eutrophic) lake or system, this refers to a less rich or even sterile body of water.

Omnivore. An animal that consumes both plant and animal material at the same time or during different seasons or at different stages in its life cycle.

pH. A scale to measure acidity (low index value) to alkalinity (higher numbers) based upon the electrical characteristics of the constituents dissolved in the water. Wetlands often range from acid (pH 4.5) to quite alkaline (pH 8.5).

Phase (of marsh vegetation cycle). Because marshes often differ dramatically in vegetation owing to water regimes, their vegetation patterns change and may be divided into phases such as drawdown-germination, emergent, submergent, and deep, open water.

Phosphorus. A chemical element essential as a component of living tissue and an essential nutrient that may limit plant productivity (hence, a common constituent of lawn and crop fertilizers).

Plankton. Small aquatic plants or animals that are suspended or may drift in the water. Plants such as algae ("phytoplankton") may be responsible for significant levels of productivity in some open marshes, and the animals ("zooplankton") include diverse microscopic protozoans and small crustaceans important as food for larger animals.

Pleistocene. A geological time period characterized by sheet glaciation in the northern United States, the most recent glaciation ranging from 8,000 to 12,000 years ago. An important influence on land forms.

Population. Usually used in reference to a collection of individuals of one species making up the residents of a prescribed area, but may be used more broadly to describe mixed species.

Pothole. A term wildlife biologists use to describe the small, shallow ponds and marshes formed by Pleistocene glaciation in the grasslands of the northern United States and southern Canada. "Kettlehole" was the original term used.

Predator. An animal that pursues and eats living animals.

Producer. An organism like a plant that produces organic manner by the natural process of nutrient and carbon dioxide intake in the presence of sunlight. Primary producers are plants that start with inorganic material and create organic tissue; secondary producers merely convert other organic tissue into animal tissue via food intake and growth.

Productivity. The end product of all producers, usually recorded as the number of gram calories produced per meter square per year.

Reservoir. An artificial body of water normally resulting from the impounding of water behind a dam. Small reservoirs also may be called impoundments.

Resource segregation. The division and use of a resource such as food by various species of animals. Reduced competition results and diversity of species probably is enhanced because they more effectively share resources.

Restoration. The returning of a wetland (or other natural habitat) to its former state by modifying conditions responsible for the loss or change. Examples include replacing a natural dam and diverting water to recreate conditions suitable for seed germination and growth of emergent plants. Natural "seed banks" often remain even after many years, and a natural setting may develop with little help.

Riverine. The channels, vegetated shallows, and bank associated with rivers, streams, and flowages.

Saline. A body of water characterized by high levels of dissolved salts. They are common in arid regions due to evaporation, and along the coasts due to the influence of ocean waters.

Seasonality. The influence of seasonal change on biological systems, such as plant growth, bird migration, and other events that are regulated by light, weather, and other seasonal events.

Section 404. A section of the Clean Water Act that gives authority to the U. S. Army Corps of Engineers to issue permits for dredging and filling in federally controlled waters.

Seed bank. A term applied by marsh ecologists and range scientists to the deposit of seeds in the soil that survive many years and that germinate when suitable conditions prevail. The durability of these seeds may make seeding unnecessary in marsh restoration and management.

Shredder. A term applied to animals of various sizes that break up vegetation into smaller parts through their feeding and cutting activities. They play an important role in the detrital cycle.

Siltation. The process whereby silt and other fine soil material accumulate in low areas or bodies of water like marshes.

Social system. The sexual and familial organization evolved by a species or group that ensures reproduction and survival of offspring, and maintenance of a viable population.

Sociobiology. The study of the social aspects of interactions of animals that influence their adaptation and survival.

Spawning. The release of eggs by fish and aquatic invertebrates in specially selected sites that provide protection and suitable conditions for hatching.

Species. A population of similar and related organisms that reproduce but that are reproductively isolated from other similar groups.

Species association. A group of intermixed species found together. It does not imply organization or obligate relationship, but is merely a description of what is present at a particular time.

Species diversity. In general usage, the term infers the number of different species found in an area. In practice by ecologists, however, it tends to infer a mathematical index (Species Diversity Index) that involves not only the number of species but relative numbers of each species as well.

Species richness. The number of species present, without reference to populations. Use of this term is preferable to species diversity to avoid confusion with the S.D.I.

Strata. Layers of vegetation of different heights above the ground. These layers create structural diversity (i.e., habitat diversity) and increase the habitats available to different species.

Succession. The process of change in plant and animal communities over time. The process can be very slow or fairly rapid. Wildlife managers commonly change habitat by manipulating succession, usually setting it back to "early" stages.

"Swimmer's itch." A rash produced by the larvae of various aquatic flukes that burrow into the human skin and die. Normally, they seek intermediate hosts like snails.

Threatened species. An uncommon to rare species given federal protection approaching that of an endangered species, but legally less restrictive on habitat protection or management.

Tide. The regular rise and fall of coastal waters produced by daily patterns of the moon's gravitational force in relation to the earth. Such changes may influence higher freshwater bodies as well, so both coastal salt- and freshwater may have tidal fluctuations.

Transpiration. The process whereby water is evaporated into the atmosphere from plant life processes. In a wetland, the amount of this water loss often exceeds that of direct evaporation of standing water.

Tundra. The vegetation zone in the far north or on high mountaintops characterized by low and non-woody vegetation that is adapted to conditions of cold, permafrost, and wind. Mosses, lichens, and sedges are prominent.

Turbidity. A measure of water clarity resulting from suspended material such as clay or algae. Measured with a secchi disk, a black-and-white-patterned or white disk lowered into the water to measure the depth to which it is visible.

Valuation. The process used by economists to place a value on a commodity. It is more difficult with items that are not for sale or that do not produce a product that can be sold or traded.

Vegetation, structure of. The physical attributes of vegetation (such as height, volume, configuration) that influence habitat appearance and diversity and attractiveness to animals.

Weed bank. An area that produces nuisance plants that may act as a source of seeds that contaminate other areas.

Wildlife Surplus. The "surplus" in wild populations above those needed to maintain the species; regarded as harvestable by hunters.

References

References

1. Adamus, P. R., and L. T. Stockwell. 1983. A method for wetland functional assessment. U.S. Dept. Transportation Federal Highway Administration Reports No. FHWA-1P, 82-23: 176 pp., and 82-24: 134 pp.
1a. Adomaitis, V. A., H. A. Kantrud, and J. A. Shoesmith, 1967. Some chemical characteristics of aeolian deposits of snow-soil on prairie wetlands. N. D. Acad. Sci. 21: 65-69.
2. Allred, E. R., P. W. Manson, G. M. Schwartz, P. Golany, and J. W. Reinke. 1971. Continuation of studies on the hydrology of ponds and small lakes, Univ. Minn. Ag. Exp. Sta. Tech. Bull. 274. 62 pp.
3. Anderson, D. R., and F. A. Glover. 1967. Effects of water manipulation on waterfowl production and habitat. Trans. N. Am. Wildl. Nat. Resour. Conf. 32:292-300.
4. Anderson, W. 1965. Waterfowl production in the vicinity of gull colonies. Calif. Fish and Game 51:5-15.
5. Andrews, N. J., and D. C. Pratt, 1978. The potential of cattails (*Typha* spp.) as an energy source: productivity in managed stands. J. Minn. Acad. Sci. 44:5-8.
6. Anonymous. 1978. Michigan introduces bill to protect wetlands. Land Use Planning Report 6:173. Business Publishers, Inc., Silver Springs, MD.
7. Anonymous. 1978. Opposition to wetlands acquisition vicious. Outdoor News Bull. 32:1-2. Wildl. Mgmt. Inst., Washington, DC.
8. Anonymous. 1980. Hunting license receipts climb. Outdoor News Bull. 34:3. Wildl. Mgmt. Inst., Washington, DC.
9. Anonymous. 1980. Wetlands. Environment Midwest, April 1980:16. Envir. Prot. Agency, Chicago, IL.
10. Anonymous. 1980. Wetlands; protecting a fragile environment. Environment Midwest, March 1980:10-15. Envir. Prot. Agency, Chicago, IL.
11. Anthony, W. E. 1975. Basic economics of drainage. Univ. Minn. Agric. Economist No. 568:3-5.
12. Atkinson, K. M. 1971. Further experiments in dispersal of phytoplankton by birds. Wildfowl Trust Ann. Rept. 22:98-99.
13. Atlantic Waterfowl Council. 1972. Techniques handbook of the waterfowl habitat development and management committee, 2nd ed. Atlantic Flyway Council, Boston, MA.

131

14. Bailey, R. M. (Ed.). 1970. A list of common and scientific names of fishes from the United States and Canada, 3rd ed. Amer. Fish. Soc. Spec. Publ. No. 6. Washington, DC. 150 pp.

15. Barney, G. O. 1980. The global 2000 report to the President, Vol. 1. U. S. Council on Environmental Quality and U. S. Dept. of State. 47 pp.

16. Bart, J., D. Allee, and M. Richmond. 1979. Using economics in defense of wildlife. Wildl. Soc. Bull. 7:139–144.

17. Beard, E. B. 1953. The importance of beaver in waterfowl management at Seney National Wildlife Refuge. J. Wildl. Mgmt. 17:398–436.

18. Beecher, W. J. 1942. Nesting birds and the vegetative substrate. Chicago Ornithological Society, Chicago, IL. 69 pp.

19. Bengtson, S. A. 1971. Variations in clutch-size in ducks in relation to the food supply. Ibis 113:523–526.

20. Bergman, R. D., R. L. Howard, K. F. Abraham, and M. W. Weller. 1977. Waterbirds and their wetland resources in relation to oil development at Storkersen Point, Alaska. U. S. Fish and Wildl. Serv. Res. Publ. 129. 38 pp.

21. Bergman, R. D., P. Swain, and M. W. Weller. 1970. A comparative study of nesting Forster's and Black Terns. Wilson Bull. 82:435–444.

22. Billington, C. 1938. The vegetation of the Cranbrook Lake bottom. Cranbrook Institute of Science, Bull. No. 11. 24 pp.

23. Bishop, R. A., R. D. Andrews, and R. J. Bridges. 1979. Marsh management and its relationship to vegetation, waterfowl and muskrats. Proc. Ia. Acad. Sci. 86:50–56.

24. Bishop, R. A., and R. Barratt. 1970. Use of artificial nest baskets by mallards. J. Wildl. Mgmt. 34:734–738.

25. Blair, C. L., and S. Sather-Blair. 1979. Highway planning coordination between resource and transportation agencies. So. Dakota Coop. Wildl. Unit, Brookings, SD. 148 pp.

26. Bossenmaier, E. F., and W. H. Marshall. 1958. Field-feeding by waterfowl in southwestern Manitoba. Wildl. Soc. Wildl. Monogr. 1. 32 pp.

27. Brenner, F. J., and J. J. Mondok. 1979. Waterfowl nesting rafts designed for fluctuating water levels. J. Wildl. Mgmt. 43:979–982.

28. Browder, J. A. 1978. A modeling study of water, wetlands, and wood storks. Pp. 325–346 *in* Wading Birds (A. Sprunt *et al*, Eds.). National Audubon Society Research Rept. No. 7, New York. 381 pp.

29. Buchsbaum, R., and M. Buchsbaum. 1957. Basic ecology. Boxwood Press, Pittsburgh, PA. 192 pp.

29a. Buech, R. R. 1985. Beaver in water impoundments: understanding a problem of water-level management. Pp. 95–105 *in* Knighton, M. D. (Ed.). Proc. of water impoundments for wildlife: a habitat management workshop, 1982. U. S. Forest Serv. North Central Forest Experiment Station. St. Paul, MN. 136 pp.

30. Cahn, A. R. 1929. The effect of carp on a small lake; the carp as a dominant. Ecol. 10:271–274.

31. Carignan, R., and J. Kalff. 1980. Phosphorous sources for aquatic weeds: water or sediments? Science 207:987–989.

32. Carter, V., M. S. Bedinger, R. P. Novitzki, and W. O. Wilen. 1979. Water resources and wetlands. Pp. 344–376 *in* Greeson, P. E., J. R. Clark, and J. E. Clark (Eds.). Wetland functions and values: the state of our understanding. Amer. Water Resources Assoc. Minneapolis, MN. 674 pp.

33. Cartwright, B. W. 1942. Regulated burning as a marsh management technique. Trans. N. Am. Wildl. Conf. 7:257–263.

34. Cartwright, B. W. 1946. Muskrats, duck production and marsh management. Trans. N. Am. Wildl. Conf. 11:454–457.

35. Catchpole, C. K., and C. F. Tydeman. 1975. Gravel pits as new wetland habitats for the conservation of breeding bird communities. Biol. Conser. 8:47–59.

36. Chabreck, R. H. 1976. Management of wetlands for wildlife habitat improvement. Pp. 226–233 *in* Wiley, M. (Ed.) Estuarine Processes, Vol. I. Academic Press, New York.

37. Chabreck, R. H. 1979. Wildlife harvest in wetlands of the United States. Pp. 618–631 *in* Greeson, P. E., J. R. Clark, and J. E. Clark (Eds.). Wetland functions and values: the state of our understanding. Amer. Water Resources Assoc. Minneapolis, MN. 674 pp.

37a. Chabreck, R. H., J. E. Holcombe, R. G. Linscombe, and N. E. Kinler. 1982. Winter foods of river otters from saline and fresh environments in Louisiana. Proc. Ann. Conf. S.E. Assoc. Fish and Wildl. Agencies 36:1–20.

38. Choate, J.S. 1972. Effects of stream channeling on wetlands in a Minnesota watershed. J. Wildl. Mgmt. 36:940–944.

39. Christiansen, J. E., and J. B. Low. 1970. Water requirements of waterfowl marshlands in northern Utah. Utah Div. of Fish & Game. No. 69–12. 108 pp.

39a. Clements, F. E. 1916. Plant succession: an analysis of the development of vegetation. Public. 242, Carnegie Institute, Washington, DC.

40. Conant, R. 1975. A field guide to reptiles and amphibians of eastern and central North America. Houghton-Mifflin Co., Boston. 429 pp.

41. Cook, A., and C. F. Powers. 1958. Early biochemical changes in the soils and waters of artificially created marshes in New York. N. Y. Fish & Game J. 5:9–65.

42. Cowardin, L. M., V. Carter, F. C. Golet, and E. T. LaRoe. 1979. Classification of wetlands and deepwater habitats of the United States. U. S. Fish and Wildl. Serv. Office of Biological Services. 103 pp.

43. Cowardin, L. M., and D. H. Johnson. 1973. A preliminary classification of wetland plant communities in north-central Minnesota. U. S. Fish and Wildl. Serv., Spec. Sci. Rep. Wildl. 168. 33 pp.

44. Crocker, W. 1938. Life span of seeds. Bot. Rev. 4:235–272.

45. Cuthbert, N. L. 1954. A nesting study of the black tern in Michigan. Auk 71:36–63.

46. Dane, C. W. 1959. Succession of aquatic plants in small artificial marshes in New York state. N. Y. Fish and Game J. 6:57–76.

47. Danell, K., and K. Sjoberg. 1977. Seasonal emergence of chironomids in relation to egglaying and hatching of ducks in a restored lake. Wildfowl 28:129–135.

48. de la Cruz, A. A. 1979. Production and transport of detritus in wetlands. Pp. 162–174 *in* Greeson, P. E., J. R. Clark, and J. E. Clark (Eds.) Wetland functions and values: the state of our understanding. Amer. Water Resources Assoc. Minneapolis, MN. 674 pp.

49. DeVlaming, V., and V. W. Proctor. 1968. Dispersal of aquatic organisms: viability of seeds recovered from the droppings of captive killdeer and mallard ducks. Am. J. Bot. 55:20–26.

50. Duebbert, H. F. 1969. The ecology of Malheur Lake. U. S. Fish and Wildl. Serv. Refuge Leaf. No. 12. 24 pp.

51. Duebbert, H. F., and J. T. Lokemoen. 1976. Duck nesting in fields of undisturbed grass-legume cover. J. Wildl. Mgmt. 40:39–49.

52. Eisenlohr, W. S., Jr., C. E. Sloan, and J. S. Shjeflo. 1972. Hydrologic investigations of prairie potholes in North Dakota, 1959–1968. Geol. Surv. Prof. Paper 585-A. 102 pp.

53. Elton, C. S. 1958. The ecology of invasions of animals and plants. Methuen, London. 181 pp.

54. Emerson, F. B. 1961. Experimental establishment of food and cover plants in marshes created for wildlife in New York State. N. Y. Fish & Game J. 8:130–144.

55. Emlen, S. T., and H. W. Ambrose, III. 1970. Feeding interactions of snowy egrets and red-breasted mergansers. Auk 87:164–165.

56. Erickson, R. E., R. L. Linder, and K. W. Harmon. 1979. Stream channelization (P.L. 33–556) increased wetland losses in the Dakotas. Wildl. Soc. Bull. 7:71–78.

57. Eriksson, M. O. G. 1978. Lake selection by Goldeneye ducklings in relation to the abundance of food. Wildfowl 29:81–85.

58. Errington, P. L. 1937. Drowning as a cause of mortality in muskrats. J. Mamm. 18:497–500.

59. Errington, P. L. 1957. Of men and marshes. Macmillan Co., New York. 150 pp.

60. Errington, P. L. 1963. Muskrat populations. Iowa State Univ. Press, Ames, Iowa. 665 pp.

61. Errington, P. L., and T. S. Scott. 1945. Reduction in productivity of muskrat pelts on an Iowa marsh through depredations of red foxes. J. Agric. Res. 71:137–148.

62. Errington, P. L., R. J. Siglin, and R. C. Clark. 1963. The decline of a muskrat population. J. Wildl. Mgmt. 27:1–8.

63. Evans, T. R. 1964. Beyond national boundaries. Pp. 717–722 *in* Linduska, J. (Ed.). Waterfowl Tomorrow. U. S. Fish and Wildl. Serv. Washington, DC. 770 pp.

64. Faaborg, J. 1976. Habitat selection and territorial behavior of the small grebes of North Dakota. Wilson Bull. 88:390–399.

64a. Farmes, R. E. 1985. So you want to build a water impoundment. Pp. 130–134 *in* Knighton, M. Dean. 1985. Proc. of water impoundments for wildlife: a habitat management workshop. U. S. Forest Serv. North Central Forest Experiment Station. St. Paul, MN. 136 pp.

65. Fassett, N. C. 1940. A manual of aquatic plants. McGraw-Hill Book Co., New York, 382 pp.

66. Flake, L. D. 1979. Wetland diversity and waterfowl. Pp. 312–319 *in* Greeson, P. E., J. R. Clark, and J. E. Clark (Eds.). Wetland functions and values: the state of our understanding. Amer. Water Resources Assoc., Minneapolis, MN. 674 pp.

67. Forney, J. L. 1968. Production of young northern pike in a regulated marsh. N. Y. Fish and Game J. 15:143–154.

68. Foster, J. H. 1979. Measuring the social value of wetland benefits. Pp. 84–92 *in* Greeson, P. E., J. R. Clark, and J. E. Clark (Eds.). Wetlands functions and values: the state of our understanding. Amer. Water Resources Assoc., Minneapolis, MN. 674 pp.

68a. Frayer, W. E., T. J. Monahan, D. C. Bowden, and F. A. Graybill. 1983. Status and trends of wetlands and deepwater habitats in the conterminous United States, 1950's to 1970's. Dept. of Forest and Wood Sciences, Colorado State University, Fort Collins. 32 pp.

68b. Fredrickson, L. H., and T. Scott Taylor. 1982. Management of seasonally flooded impoundments for wildlife. U. S. Fish and Wildl. Serv. Resour. Publ. 148, Washington, DC. 29 pp.

69. Fritzell, P. A. 1979. American wetlands as cultural symbol: place of wetlands in American culture. Pp. 523–534 *in* Greeson, P. E., J. R. Clark, and J. E. Clark (Eds.). Wetland functions and values: the state of our understanding. Amer. Water Resources Assoc., Minneapolis, MN. 674 pp.

70. Gale, W. F. 1975. Bottom fauna of a segment of Pool 19, Mississippi River, near Fort Madison, Iowa, 1967–1968. Ia. St. J. Res. 49:353–372.

71. Ganning, B., and F. Wulff. 1969. The effects of bird droppings on chemical and biological dynamics in brackish water rockpools. Oikos 20:274–289.

72. Gasaway, R. D., and T. F. Drda. 1977. Effects of grass carp introduction on waterfowl habitat. Trans. No. Amer. Wildl. Nat. Resour. Conf. 42:73–85.

73. Geis, J. W. 1979. Shoreline processes affecting the distribution of wetland habitat. Trans. N. Am. Wildl. Nat. Resour. Conf. 44:529–542.

74. Giles, R. H., Jr. (Ed.). 1969. Wildlife Management Techniques, 3rd ed., revised. The Wildlife Society, Washington, DC. 623 pp.

74a. Gleason, H. A. 1917. The structure and development of the plant association. Bull. Torrey Bot. Club 44:463–481.

75. Golet, F. C., and J. S. Larson. 1974. Classification of freshwater wetlands in the glaciated northeast. U. S. Fish and Wildl. Serv. Res. Publ. 116. 56 pp.

76. Good, R. E., D. F. Whigham, and R. L. Simpson (Eds.). 1978. Freshwater wetlands; ecological processes and management potential. Academic Press, New York. 378 pp.

77. Goss, W. L. 1924. The viability of buried seeds. J. Agric. Res. 29:349–362.

78. Gosselink, J. C., E. P. Odum, and R. M. Pope. 1973. The value of the tidal marsh. Public. No. LSU-SG-74-03. Center for Wetland Resources, Baton Rouge, LA. 30 pp.

79. Greeson, P. E., J. R. Clark, and J. E. Clark (Eds.). 1979. Wetland functions and values; the state of our understanding. Amer. Water Resources Assoc., Minneapolis, MN. 674 pp.

80. Gupta, R. R., and J. H. Foster. 1975. Economics criteria for freshwater wetland policy in Massachusetts. Am. J. Agric. Econ. 57:40–45.

81. Hammack, J., and G. M. Brown, Jr. 1974. Waterfowl and Wetlands: Toward Bioeconomic Analysis. Johns Hopkins Univ. Press, Baltimore. 95 pp.

82. Harmon, K. W. 1979. Mitigating losses of private wetlands: the North Dakota situation. Pp. 157–163 *in* Swanson, G. A. (Ed.). The mitigation symposium. Gen. Tech. Rept. RM-65, U. S. Forest Serv. Rocky Mtn. For. and Range Exp. Sta., Ft. Collins, CO. 684 pp.

83. Harris, S. W., and W. H. Marshall. 1960. Germination and planting experiments on soft-stem and hard-stem bulrush. J. Wildl. Mgmt. 24:134–139.

84. Harris, S. W., and W. H. Marshall. 1963. Ecology of water-level manipulations of a northern marsh. Ecol. 44:331–342.

85. Harrison, J. 1970. Creating a wetland habitat. Bird Study 17:111–122.

86. Harter, R. D. 1966. The effect of water levels on soil chemistry and plant growth of the Ma-gee Marsh Wildlife Area. Ohio Dept. Nat. Res. Game Monogr. No. 2. 36 pp.

87. Have, M. R. 1973. Effects of migratory waterfowl on water quality at the Montezuma National Wildlife Refuge, Seneca County, New York. Jour. Research U. S. Geol. Surv. 1:725–734.

88. Heding, R. 1964. Game fish nurseries. WI. Conserv. Bull. 29:7.

89. Hewitt, O. H. 1967. A road-count index to breeding populations of Red-winged Blackbirds. J. Wildl. Mgmt. 31:39–47.

90. Hochbaum, H. A. 1944. The canvasback on a prairie marsh. Amer. Wildl. Inst., Washington, DC.

91. Hoffpauir, C. M. 1968. Burning for coastal marsh management. Pp. 134–139 *in* Newson, J. (Ed.). Proc. of the marsh and estuary management symposium. Baton Rouge, LA.

92. Hohman, W. L. 1977. Invertebrate habitat preferences in several contiguous Minnesota wetlands. M.S. thesis, U. of North Dakota, Fargo. 79 pp.

93. Horwitz, E. L. 1978. Our nation's wetlands—an interagency task force report. U. S. Govt. Printing Office, Washington, DC. 70 pp.

94. Hotchkiss, N. 1970. Common marsh plants of the United States and Canada. U. S. Fish and Wildl. Serv. Res. Publ. 93. Washington, DC. 99 pp.

95. Jaworski, E., and C. N. Raphael. 1979. Mitigation of fish and wildlife habitat losses in Great Lakes coastal wetlands. Pp. 152–156 *in* Swanson, G. A. (Ed.). The mitigation symposium. Gen. Tech. Rept. RM-65, U. S. Forest Serv. Rocky Mtn. For. and Range Exp. Sta., Ft. Collins, CO. 684 pp.

96. Jaworski, E., and C. N. Raphael. 1979. Historical changes in natural diversity of freshwater wetlands, glaciated region of northern United States. Pp. 545–557 *in* Greeson, P. E., J. R. Clark, and J. E. Clark (Eds.). Wetland functions and values: the state of our understanding. Amer. Water Resources Assoc., Minneapolis, MN. 674 pp.

97. Jeglum, J. K., A. N. Boissonneau, and V. F. Haavisto. 1974. Toward a wetland classification for Ontario. Can. For. Serv., Sault Ste. Marie, Ont. Inf. Rep. O-X-215. 54 pp.

98. Joyner, D. E. 1980. Influence of invertebrates on pond selection by ducks in Ontario. J. Wildl. Mgmt. 44:700–705.

99. Kadlec, J. A. 1962. Effects of a drawdown on a waterfowl impoundment. Ecol. 43: 267–281.

100. Kadlec, J. A. 1979. Nitrogen and phosphorus dynamics in inland freshwater wetlands. Pp. 17–41 *in* Bookout, T. A. (Ed.). Waterfowl and Wetlands—an integrated review. Proc. of a symposium of the 39th Fish and Wildl. Conf. Madison, WI. 1977.

101. Kadlec, R. H. 1979. Wetlands for tertiary treatment. Pp. 490–504 *in* Greeson, P. E., J. R. Clark, and J. E. Clark (Eds.). Wetland functions and values: the state of our understanding. Amer. Water Resources Assoc., Minneapolis, MN. 674 pp.

102. Kadlec, R. H., and J. A. Kadlec. 1979. Wetlands and water quality. Pp. 436–456 *in* Greeson, P. E., J. R. Clark, and J. E. Clark (Eds.). Wetland functions and values: the state of our understanding. Amer. Water Resources Assoc., Minneapolis, MN. 674 pp.

103. Kaminski, R. M., and H. H. Prince. 1981. Dabbling duck activity and foraging response to aquatic macroinvertebrates. Auk 98:115–126.

104. Keith, L. B. 1964. Some social and economic values of the recreational use of Horicon Marsh, Wisconsin. Univ. Wisc. Res. Bull. 246. 16 pp.

105. Kellert, S. R. 1979. Public attitudes toward critical wildlife and natural habitat issues; Phase I. Nat. Tech. Inform. Serv., PB 80-138332. 138 pp. U. S. Dept. Commerce, Washington, DC.

106. Kendeigh, S. C. 1961. Animal Ecology. Prentice-Hall, Inc., Englewood Cliffs, NJ. 468 pp.

107. Kiel, W. H., Jr., A. S. Hawkins, and N. G. Perret. 1972. Waterfowl habitat trends in the aspen parkland of Manitoba. Can. Wildl. Serv. Rept. Ser. 18. 61 pp.

108. King, D. R., and G. S. Hunt. 1967. Effect of carp on vegetation in a Lake Erie marsh. J. Wildl. Mgmt. 31:181–188.

109. Kirsch, L. M. 1969. Waterfowl production in relation to grazing. J. Wildl. Mgmt. 33:821–828.

110. Kleinert, S. J. 1970. Production of northern pike in a managed marsh. Lake Ripley, Wisconsin. WI. Dept. Nat. Res. Rept. 49. 19 pp.

110a. Knighton, M. Dean. 1985. Proc. of water impoundments for wildlife: a habitat management workshop. U. S. Forest Serv. North Central Forest Experiment Station. St. Paul, MN. 136 pp.

111. Koskimies, J. 1957. Terns and gulls as features of habitat recognition for birds nesting in their colonies. Ornis Fennica 34:1–6.

112. Krapu, G. L. 1974. Feeding ecology of pintail hens during reproduction. Auk 91:278–290.

113. Krapu, G. L. 1979. Nutrition of female dabbling ducks during reproduction. Pp. 59–70 *in* Bookout, T. A. (Ed.). Waterfowl and Wetlands – an integrated review. Proc. of a symposium of the 39th Fish and Wildl. Conf. Madison, WI. 1977.

114. Krapu, G. L., and H. F. Duebbert. 1974. A biological survey of Kraft Slough. Prairie Naturalist 6:33–55.

115. Krapu, G. L., D. R. Parsons, and M. W. Weller. 1970. Waterfowl in relation to land use and water levels on the Spring Run area. Ia. St. J. Sci. 44:437–452.

116. Krecker, F. H. 1939. A comparative study of the animal population of certain submerged aquatic plants. Ecol. 20:553–562.

117. Krummes, W. T. 1941. The muskrat: A factor in waterfowl habitat management. Trans. N. Am. Wildl. Conf. 5:395–398.

118. Kubichek, W. F. 1940. Collecting and storing seeds of waterfowl food plants for propagation. Trans. N. Am. Wildl. Conf. 5:364–368.

118a. Kushlan, J. A. 1974. Quantitative sampling of fish populations in shallow, freshwater environments. Trans. Am. Fish. Soc. 103:348–352.

118b. Kusler, J. A. 1983. Our national wetland heritage. Environmental Law Institute. Washington, DC. 167 pp.

119. Lagler, K. F. 1956. The pike, *Esox lucius* Linnaeus, in relation to waterfowl on the Seney National Wildlife Refuge, Michigan. J. Wildl. Mgmt. 20:114–124.

120. Larson, J. S. 1971. Progress toward a decision-making model for public management of freshwater wetlands. Trans. N. Am. Wildl. Nat. Resour. Conf. 36:376–382.

121. Larson, J. S. 1975. Evaluation models for public management of freshwater wetlands. Trans. N. Am. Wildl. Nat. Resour. Conf. 40:220–228.

122. Leitch, J. A., and L. E. Danielson. 1979. Social, economic and institutional incentives to drain or preserve prairie wetlands. U. Minn. Dept. Agric. and Appl. Econ., Rept. EC79-6. 78 pp.

123. Linde, A. F. 1969. Techniques for wetlands management. WI. Dept. Nat. Res. Rept. 45. 156 pp.

124. Linde, A. F., T. Janisch, and D. Smith. 1976. Cattail – the significance of its growth, phenology, and carbohydrate storage to its control and management. WI. Dept. Nat. Resour. Tech. Bull. 94. 27 pp.

125. Lingle, G. R., and N. F. Sloan. 1980. Food habits of White Pelicans during 1976 and 1977 at Chase Lake National Wildlife Refuge, North Dakota. Wilson Bull. 92:123-125.

126. Livingston, R. J., and O. L. Loucks. 1979. Productivity, trophic interactions, and foodweb relationships in wetlands and associated systems. Pp. 101-119 *in* Greeson, P. E., J. R. Clark, and J. E. Clark (Eds.). Wetland functions and values: the state of our understanding. Amer. Water Resources Assoc., Minneapolis, MN. 674 pp.

127. Lueschow, L. A. 1972. Biology and control of aquatic nuisances in recreational waters. WI. Dept. Nat. Resour. Tech. Bull. 57. 35 pp.

128. MacBride, T. H. 1909. The geology of Hamilton and Wright Counties. Ia. Geol. Surv. 20:101-138.

129. Madson, R. 1980. Prairie wetlands; a resource threatened. No. Midwest Reg. Audubon Newsletter 2:1-2.

130. Malone, C. R. 1965. Dispersal of aquatic gastropods via the intestinal tract of water birds. Nautilus 78:135-139.

131. Mann, G. E. 1955. Wetlands inventory of Iowa. Office of River Basins Studies Report, U. S. Fish and Wildlife Service, Region IV. Minneapolis, MN. 41 pp. + 27 pp. appendix.

132. Manny, B. A., R. G. Wetzel, and W. C. Johnson. 1975. Annual contribution of carbon, nitrogen, and phosphorus by migrant Canada Geese to a hardwater lake. Verh. Internat. Verein. Limnol. 19:945-951.

133. Martin, A. C., R. E. Erickson, and J. H. Steenis. 1957. Improving duck marshes by weed control. U. S. Fish and Wildl. Serv. Circ. 19-Revised. 60 pp. Washington, DC.

134. Martin, A. C., N. Hotchkiss, F. M. Uhler, and W. S. Bourn. 1953. Classification of wetlands of the United States. U. S. Fish and Wildl. Serv., Spec. Sci. Rep. Wildl. 20. 14 pp.

135. Mathiak, H. A., and A. F. Linde. 1956. Studies on level ditching for marsh management. WI. Con. Dept. Tech. Wildl. Bull. 12. 48 pp.

136. Maxwell, G. 1957. People of the reeds. Pyramid Publications, New York.

137. McAndrews, J. H., R. E. Stewart, Jr., and R. C. Bright. 1967. Paleoecology of a prairie pothole; a preliminary report. Pp. 101-113 *in* Clayton, Lee, and Freers (Eds.). Midwestern Friends of the Pleistocene Guidebook, 18th Ann. Field Conf. N. D. Geol. Surv. Misc. Ser. 30.

138. Meanley, B. 1971. Blackbirds and the southern rice crop. U. S. Fish Wildl. Serv. Res. Publ. 100. 64 pp. Washington, DC.

139. Meeks, R. L. 1969. The effect of drawdown date on wetland plant succession. J. Wildl. Mgmt. 33:817-821.

140. Millar, J. B. 1971. Shoreline-area as a factor in rate of water loss from small sloughs. J. Hydrol. 14:259-284.

141. Millar, J. B. 1973. Vegetation changes in shallow marsh wetlands under improving moisture regime. Can. J. Bot. 51:1443-1457.

142. Millar, J. B. 1976. Wetland classification in western Canada: A guide to marshes and shallow open water wetlands in the grasslands and parklands of the Prairie Provinces. Can. Wildl. Serv. Rep. Ser. 37. 38 pp.

143. Miller, R. B., and R. C. Thomas. 1956. Alberta's pothole trout fisheries. Tran. Am. Fish. Soc. 86:261-268.

144. Momot, W. T., and H. Gowing. 1978. The dynamics of crayfish and their role in ecosystems. Am. Midl. Nat. 99:10-35.

145. Moore, I. D., and C. L. Larson. 1979. Effects of drainage projects on surface runoff from small depressional watersheds in the North Central Region. Univ. Minn. Water Resources Res. Center Bull. 99. 225 pp.

146. Moyle, J. B., and N. Hotchkiss. 1945. The aquatic waterfowl and marsh vegetation of Minnesota and its value to waterfowl. MN. Dept. Conserv. Tech. Bull. 3. 122 pp.

147. Needham, J. G., and P. R. Needham. 1941. A guide to the study of freshwater biology. Comstock Publ., Co., Ithaca, NY. 89 pp.

148. Nelson, N. F., and R. H. Dietz. 1966. Cattail control methods in Utah. Utah State Dept. of Fish and Game Publ. No. 66-2. 31 pp.

149. Nichols, S. A. 1974. Mechanical and habitat manipulation for aquatic plant management. WI. Dept. Nat. Resour. Tech. Bull. 77. 34 pp.

150. Nickell, W. P. 1966. Common Terns nest on muskrat lodges and floating cattail mats. Wilson Bull. 78:123–124.

150a. Niering, W. A. 1985. Wetlands. The Audubon Nature Guide Series. Alfred A. Knopf, Inc. New York, NY. 638 pp.

151. Novitzki, R. P. 1979. Hydrologic characteristics of Wisconsin's wetlands and their influence on floods, stream flow, and sediment. Pp. 377–388 *in* Greeson, P. E., J. R. Clark, and J. E. Clark (Eds.). Wetland functions and values: the state of our understanding. Amer. Water Resources Assoc., Minneapolis, MN. 674 pp.

152. Nutting, W. B. 1966. Biology of a pond. Amer. Biol. Teacher 28:351–360.

153. Odum, E. P. 1971. Fundamentals of ecology. W. B. Saunders Co., Philadelphia, PA. 574 pp.

154. Orians, G. H. 1961. The ecology of blackbird (*Agelaius*) social systems. Ecol. Monogr. 31:285–312.

155. Orians, G. H., and H. S. Horn. 1969. Overlap in foods of four species of blackbirds in the potholes of central Washington. Ecol. 50:930–938.

156. Ortego, B., R. B. Hamilton, and R. E. Noble. 1976. Bird usage by habitat types in a large freshwater lake. S. E. Assoc. Game and Fish Comm. 13:627–633.

157. Osvald, S., and C. W. Belin. 1979. Corps permit processing. Pp. 50–56 *in* Greeson, P. E., J. R. Clark, and J. E. Clark (Eds.). Wetland functions and values: the state of our understanding. Amer. Water Resources Assoc., Minneapolis, MN. 674 pp.

158. Ovington, J. D., and W. H. Pearsall. 1956. Production ecology II. Shoot production in *Phragmites* in relation to habitat. Oikos 7:206–214.

159. Paterson, C. G., and C. H. Fernando. 1971. A comparison of a simple corer and an Ekman grab for sampling shallow-water benthos. J. Fish. Res. Bd. Canada 28:365–368.

160. Patterson, J. H. 1976. The role of environmental heterogeneity in the regulation of duck populations. J. Wildl. Mgmt. 40:22–32.

161. Pennak, R. W. 1978. Fresh-water invertebrates of the United States. 2nd ed. John Wiley, New York. 803 pp.

162. Priegel, G. R. 1970. Reproduction and early life history of the walleye in the Lake Winnebago Region. WI. Dept. Nat. Resour. Tech. Bull. 45. 105 pp.

163. Provost, M. W. 1947. Nesting birds in the marshes of northwest Iowa. Am. Midl. Nat. 38:485–503.

164. Provost, M. W. 1948. Marsh-blasting as a wildlife management technique. J. Wildl. Mgmt. 12:350–387.

165. Quade, H. W. 1969. Cladoceran faunas associated with aquatic macrophytes in some lakes in Northwestern Minnesota. Ecol. 50:170–179.

166. Ranwell, D. S. 1967. Introduced aquatic, fresh-water and salt marsh—case histories and ecological effects. Proc. & Papers IUCN Tech. Mtg. 10, IUCN Publ. New Series No. 9:27–37.

167. Reichholf, J. 1976. The possible use of the aquatic bird communities as indicators for the ecological conditions of wetlands. Landschaft Stadt. 8:125–129.

168. Reid, G. K. 1961. Ecology of inland waters and estuaries. D. Van Nostrand Co., New York. 375 pp.

169. Richardson, C. 1979. Primary productivity values in fresh water wetlands. Pp. 131–145 *in* Greeson, P. E., J. R. Clark, and J. E. Clark (Eds.). Wetland functions and values: the state of our understanding. Amer. Water Resources Assoc., Minneapolis, MN. 674 pp.

170. Robel, R. J. 1961. The effect of carp populations on the production of waterfowl food plants on a western waterfowl marsh. Trans. N. Am. Wildl. Conf. 26:147–159.

171. Robel, R. J. 1961. Water depth and turbidity in relation to growth of Sago Pondweed. J. Wildl. Mgmt. 25:436–438.

172. Robel, R. J. 1962. Changes in submersed vegetation following a change in water level. J. Wildl. Mgmt. 26:221–224.

173. Rogers, J. P. 1959. Low water and lesser scaup reproduction near Erickson, Manitoba. Trans. N. Am. Wildl. Conf. 24:216–224.

174. Rogers, J. P., J. D. Nichols, F. W. Martin, and C. F. Kimball. 1979. An examination of harvest and survival rates of ducks in relation to hunting. Trans. N. Am. Wildl. Nat. Resour. Conf.44:114–126.

175. Rosenbaum, N. 1979. Enforcing wetlands regulations. Pp. 43–49 *in* Greeson, P. E., J. R. Clark, and J. E. Clark (Eds.). Wetland functions and values: the state of our understanding. Amer. Water Resources Assoc., Minneapolis, MN. 674 pp.

176. Rosine, W. N. 1955. The distribution of invertebrates on submerged aquatic plant surfaces in Muskee Lake, Colorado. Ecol. 36:308–314.

177. Ryther, J. H., T. A. DeBusk, M. D. Hanisak, and L. D. Williams. 1979. Fresh water macrophytes for energy and waste water treatment. Pp. 652–660 *in* Greeson, P. E., J. R. Clark, and J. E. Clark (Eds.). Wetland functions and values: the state of our understanding. Amer. Water Resources Assoc., Minneapolis, MN. 674 pp.

178. Schindler, D. W. 1974. Eutrophication and recovery in experimental lakes: implications for lake management. Science 184:897–899.

178a. Schnick, R. A., J. M. Morton, J. C. Mochalski, and J. T. Beall (Eds.). 1982. Greentree reservoirs and mast management. Pp. 418–425 *in*: Mitigation and enhancement techniques for the upper Mississippi River system and other large river systems. U. S. Fish and Wildl. Serv. Resource Publ. 149. Washington, DC. 714 pp.

179. Schroeder, L. D. 1973. A literature review on the role of invertebrates in waterfowl management. Colorado Div. Wildl. Spec. Rep. No. 29. 13 pp.

180. Schroeder, L. D., D. R. Anderson, R. S. Pospahala, G. W. Robinson, and F. A. Glover. 1976. Effects of early water application on waterfowl production. J. Wildl. Mgmt. 40: 227–232.

181. Scott, T. G., and W. L. Dever. 1940. Blasting to improve wildlife environment in marshes. J. Wildl. Mgmt. 4:373–374.

182. Scott, T. G., and C. H. Wasser. 1980. Checklist of North American Plants for Wildlife Biologists. Wildlife Soc., Washington, DC. 58 pp.

183. Sculthorpe, C. D. 1967. The biology of aquatic vascular plants. Edward Arnold, Ltd., London. 610 pp.

184. Sealy, S. G. 1978. Clutch size and nest placement of the Pied-billed Grebe in Manitoba. Wilson Bull. 90:301–302.

185. Seamans, R. 1959. An illustrated small marsh construction manual based on standard designs. Com. Habitat Mgt. and Devel., Atl. Waterfowl Council, Vt. Fish and Game Serv. 157 pp.

186. Shaw, S. P., and C. G. Fredine. 1956. Wetlands of the United States. U. S. Fish and Wildl. Serv. Circ. 39:67 pp. Washington, DC.

187. Shearer, L. A., B. J. Jahn, and L. Lenz. 1969. Deterioration of duck foods when flooded. J. Wildl. Mgmt. 33:1012–1015.

188. Shull, G. H. 1914. The longevity of submerged seed. Plant World 17:329–337.

189. Sloan, C. E. 1972. Ground-water hydrology of prairie potholes in North Dakota. U.S. Geol. Surv. Prof. Paper 585-C. 28 pp.

190. Sloey, W. E., F. L. Spangler, and C. W. Fetter, Jr. 1978. Management of freshwater wetlands for nutrient assimilation. Pp. 321–340 *in* Good, R. E., F. G. Whigham, and R. L. Simpson (Eds.). Freshwater Wetlands: Ecological Processes and Management Potential. Academic Press, New York. 378 pp.

191. Smith, R. H. 1964. Experimental control of purple loosestrife (*Lythrum Salicaria*). N. Y. Fish & Game J. 11:35–46.

192. Smith, R. I. 1970. Response of pintail breeding populations to drought. J. Wildl. Mgmt. 34:943–946.

193. Stearns, L. A., D. MacCreasy, and F. C. Daigh. 1940. Effect of ditching for mosquito con-

trol on the muskrats of a Delaware tidal marsh. Univ. of Delaware Agric. Exp. Sta. Bull. No. 225. 55 pp.

194. Stewart, R. E., and H. A. Kantrud. 1971. Classification of natural ponds and lakes in the glaciated prairie region. U. S. Fish and Wildl. Serv. Res. Publ. 92. 57 pp.

195. Stewart, R. E., and H. A. Kantrud. 1972. Vegetation of prairie potholes, North Dakota, in relation to quality of water and other environmental factors. U. S. Geol. Surv. Prof. Paper 585-D. 36 pp.

196. Stewart, R. E., and H. A. Kantrud. 1973. Ecological distribution of breeding waterfowl populations in North Dakota. J. Wildl. Mgmt. 37:39-50.

197. Stewart, R. E., and H. A. Kantrud. 1974. Breeding waterfowl populations in the prairie pothole region of North Dakota. Condor 76:70-79.

198. Stone, C. P., and D. F. Mott. 1973. Bird damage to ripening field corn in the United States, 1971. U. S. Fish and Wildl. Serv. Wildl. Leaflet 505:1-8. Washington, DC.

199. Strohmeyer, D. L., and L. H. Fredrickson. 1967. An evaluation of dynamited potholes in Northwest Iowa. J. Wildl. Mgmt. 31:525-532.

200. Sugden, L. G. 1978. Canvasback habitat use and production in Saskatchewan parklands. Can. Wildl. Serv. Occas. Paper No. 34. 30 pp.

201. Sugden, L. G., and D. A. Benson. 1970. An evaluation of loafing rafts for attracting ducks. J. Wildl. Mgmt. 34:340-343.

202. Swanson, G. A., and M. I. Meyer. 1973. The role of invertebrates in the feeding ecology of Anatinae during the breeding season. Pp. 143-185 *in* The Waterfowl Habitat Manage. Symp. Moncton, New Brunswick. 306 pp.

203. Swanson, G. A., and M. I. Meyer. 1977. Impact of fluctuating water levels on feeding ecology of breeding blue-winged teal. J. Wildl. Mgmt. 41:426-433.

204. Swanson, G. A., and H. K. Nelson. 1970. Potential influence of fish rearing programs on waterfowl breeding habitat. *In* Schneberger E. (Ed.). A symposium on the management of Midwestern winterkill lakes. North Central Div. Am. Fish. Soc. in Conjunction with 32nd Midwest Fish and Wildl. Conf. Winnipeg, Manitoba, Canada.

205. Swindale, D. N., and J. T. Curtis. 1957. Phytosociology of the larger submerged plants in Wisconsin Lakes. Ecol. 38:397-407.

206. Teal, J., and M. Teal. 1969. Life and death of the salt marsh. Audubon/Ballantine Books, New York. 274 pp.

207. Threinen, C. W., and W. T. Helm. 1954. Experiments and observations designed to show carp destruction of aquatic vegetation. J. Wildl. Mgmt. 18:247-251.

207a. Tiner, R. W., Jr. 1984. Wetlands of the United States: Current status and recent trends. U. S. Fish and Wildlife Service, National Wetlands Inventory. 59 pp.

208. Toburen, C. 1974. Reclaiming Boulder County gravel pit as a wildlife area. Boulder Valley Soil Cons. Dist., Boulder, CO. 41 pp.

209. Trauger, D. L., and J. H. Stoudt. 1978. Trends in waterfowl populations and habitats on study areas in Canadian parklands. Trans. N. Am. Wildl. Nat. Resour. Conf. 43:187-205.

210. Tryon, C. A., Jr. 1954. The effect of carp exclosures on growth of submerged aquatic vegetation in Pymatuning Lake, Pennsylvania. J. Wildl. Mgmt. 18:251-254.

211. Uhler, M. M. 1956. New habitats for waterfowl. Trans. N. Am. Wildl. Conf. 21:453-469.

212. Utschick, H. 1976. Die Wasservögel als Indikatoren für den ökologischen Zustand von Seen. Verh. orn. Ges. Bayer 22:395-438.

212a. van der Valk, A. G. 1981. Succession in wetlands: A Gleasonian approach. Ecology 62:688-696.

213. van der Valk, A. G., and C. B. Davis. 1978. The role of seed banks in the vegetation dynamics of prairie glacial marshes. Ecol. 59:322-335.

214. van der Valk, A. G., C. B. Davis, J. L. Baker, and C. E. Beer. 1979. Natural fresh water wetlands as Nitrogen and Phosphorus traps for land runoff. Pp. 457-467 *in* Greeson, P. E.,

J. R. Clark, and J. E. Clark (Eds.). Wetland functions and values: the state of our understanding. Amer. Water Resources Assoc., Minneapolis, MN. 674 pp.

215. Vermeer, K. 1968. Ecological aspects of ducks nesting in high densities among Larids. Wilson Bull. 80:78–83.

216. Voigts, D. K. 1973. Food niche overlap of two Iowa marsh icterids. Condor 75:392–399.

217. Voigts, D. K. 1976. Aquatic invertebrate abundance in relation to changing marsh vegetation. Am. Midl. Nat. 95:312–322.

218. Ward, E. 1942. Phragmites management. Trans. N. Am. Wildl. Conf. 7:294–298.

219. Ward, H. B., and G. C. Whipple. 1959. Freshwater biology. W. Edmondson (Ed.). John Wiley and Sons, New York. 1248 pp.

220. Ward, P. 1968. Fire in relation to waterfowl habitat of the Delta marshes. Proceedings Tall Timbers Fire Ecology Conf. 8:254–267.

221. Weller, M. W. 1972. Ecological studies of Falkland Islands' waterfowl. Wildfowl 23:25–44.

222. Weller, M. W. 1975. Studies of cattail in relation to management for marsh wildlife. Ia. St. J. Sci. 49:383–412.

223. Weller, M. W. 1978. Management of freshwater marshes for wildlife. Pp. 267–284 *in* Good, R. E., D. F. Whigham, and R. L. Simpson (Eds.). Freshwater wetlands, ecological processes and management potential. Academic Press, New York. 378 pp.

224. Weller, M. W. 1979. Birds of some Iowa wetlands in relation to concepts of faunal preservation. Proc. Ia. Acad. Sci. 86:81–88.

225. Weller, M. W., and L. H. Fredrickson. 1974. Avian ecology of a managed glacial marsh. The Living Bird 12:269–291.

226. Weller, M. W., and C. E. Spatcher. 1965. Role of habitat in the distribution and abundance of marsh birds. Iowa St. Univ. Agric. and Home Econ. Exp. Sta. Spec. Rept. No. 43. 31 pp.

227. Weller, M. W., B. H. Wingfield, and J. B. Low. 1958. Effects of habitat deterioration on bird populations of a small Utah marsh. Condor 60:220–226.

228. Wentz, W. A., R. L. Smith, and J. A. Kadlec. 1974. State-of-the-art survey and evaluation of marsh plant establishment techniques: induced and natural; volume II, a selected annotated bibliography on aquatic and marsh plants and their management. U. S. Army Engineers Waterways Experiment Station, Vicksburg, MS. 206 pp.

229. Wetzel, R. G. 1975. Limnology. W. B. Saunders Co., Philadelphia, PA. 658 pp.

230. White, D. A. 1966. Vegetative spreading of cattails through carp disturbance. Am. Midl. Nat. 76:510.

231. Willson, M. F. 1966. Breeding ecology of the Yellow-headed Blackbird. Ecol. Monogr. 36:51–77.

231a. Zagata, M. D. 1985. Mitigation banking by "credits": A Louisiana pilot project. Trans. N. Am. Wildl. Nat. Resour. Conf. 50:475-485.

Index

Index

Airboat, 114
Alaska, viii, 44, 104
Algae, 30, 49
Alkali, 12
Alligator, 11, 46
Amphibian, 38, 45, 46, 49, 118
Anaerobic, 70, 100
Animal:
    adaptations, 31–34;
    populations, 104, 113;
    response to habitat, 54;
    sounds, 34
Aquaculture, 83
Argentina, 42
Arkansas, 95
Arrowhead, 20, 26, 56
Arthropod, 40

Backswimmers, 48
Bacteria, 26, 56
Barley, 95
Basin (marsh), 3, 7, 12, 18, 23, 56, 78–79
Beaver, 11, 42, 55
Beetle, 49
Benthic, 49, 117
Biomass, 4, 101
Birds: 36–41, 49, 64, 82, 96;
    alarm call, 34;
    breeding, 52, 81, 119;
    development, 48;
    food, 62;

habitat, 62, 64;
movements, 52, 55;
nests, 64;
sampling, 117–118;
social system, 33, 34, 41, 104;
song perch, 32, 118;
species richness, 117;
winter, 114;
yearling, 52
Bison, 78
Bittern, 34, 39, 46, 98
Blackbird, 23, 24, 27, 32–34, 37, 40, 41, 52, 64, 93–98, 114
Bladderwort, 21
Bloodworms, 48
Boating, 83, 98, 107, 114
Bog, 3, 9, 11, 14, 78
Botanist, 5
British Columbia, 104
Bug (Hemiptera), 48
Bulldozer, 79
Bulrush, 3, 21, 26, 39, 56, 58
Bureau of Land Management, 108

Cactus, 40
Caddis flies, 49, 117
California, 95
Canoeing, 107, 114
Canvasback, 39, 66, 89, 119
Capillary action, 13
Carnivore, 25, 37, 41, 43

Carp, 11, 19, 45, 57, 74, 84
Cattail, 3, 13, 19, 26, 29, 35, 39, 52, 56,
    58, 79, 101, 102, 120
Clam, 33, 50
Clean Water Act, 109
Climate, 101–102
Climatologist, 5
Coal mining, 82
Community, viii, 23, 26, 104
Competition, 32, 33, 56, 83–85, 103
Conductivity, 116
Consumers, 25, 32, 44, 45
Coots, 24, 40, 52, 66, 77, 79, 98
Copepod, 49
Corn, 94, 95
Cottonwood, 56, 120
Crane, 89, 104
Crane fly, 47
Crayfish, 11, 35, 43, 44, 49
Crustacean, 26, 31, 47, 49
Curlew, 89
Cutgrass, 21
Cyclops, 49

Dam, 74, 98, 108
Damselflies, 48, 117
Daphnia, 49
Decomposition, 29, 95
Deer, 35, 114
Delta Waterfowl Research Station, viii, 87
Department of Agriculture, 108
Detritivores, 25, 29, 50
Diptera, 47
Diver (or loon), 37
Diversity of life, 4–5, 17
Dove, 66
Dragonflies, 31, 47, 48, 53, 117
Drainage, 53, 81, 88, 98, 108
Drawdown, 75–77, 83, 121
Dredge, 108, 117
Drought, 54, 58
Duck: 7, 23, 24, 46, 48, 81, 93, 95, 121;
    dabbling, 32, 37, 77, 78, 119, 120;
    diving, 70, 77, 79, 98, 120, 121;
    fulvous whistling, 39;
    harvest, 103;
    loafing site, 118;
    mallard, 33, 35, 80, 89, 92;
    mortality, 70;
    nesting, 78

ruddy, 39;
    wood, 24, 81
Duck potato, 119
Duck stamp, 73
Ducks Unlimited, 73, 87
Duckweed, 22, 30

Ecologist, 5
Economist, 92
Ecosystem, viii, 4, 25–30, 36
Ecotone (edge), 24, 35
Education, public, 107–108
Eggs, 31, 33, 81–82
Egret, 23, 33, 39, 40
Eider, 33
Elephant, 11
Endangered species, 103–104, 111
Energy, viii, 101, 102
Engineer, 74, 88, 101, 108, 109, 111
Entomologist, 5
Environmental concerns, 102
Environmental impact statement, 109
Environmental Protection Agency, 109
Erosion, 89
Errington, Paul L., 62, 98
Europe, 102
Eutrophy, 28, 30, 45, 53, 72
Evaporation, 12
Evolution, 36, 100
Exotics, 84–85

Farmland, 38, 81
Fen, 14
Fertilizer, 78, 101
Fire, 74, 78
Fish, 18, 19, 27, 33, 38, 40, 42–45, 48, 49,
    53, 56, 70, 83, 84, 103, 108
Fish and Wildlife Service, 73, 91 108
Fish sampling, 118
Flies, 47
Flood, 10, 58, 89, 93, 109, 120
Florida: 42, 101, 111;
    Everglades, 92–93, 104, 107, 114
Food, 25–28, 44, 47, 49, 52, 58, 67–70
Fox, 52, 58, 106
Frog, 34, 35, 39, 43, 45, 46, 48, 68
Fungi, 26, 56
Furbearers, 26, 79, 103

Gadwall, 79

Gallinule, 40
Geese, 37, 39, 79, 89
Geologist, 5
Georgia, 109
Germination, 42, 56, 75, 81
Glacial, 7, 8, 74
Goose, Canada, 32, 79, 80
Great Basin, viii, 10
Great Lakes, 9, 88
Great Salt Lake, 10
Grebes, 28, 33, 34, 36–38, 66, 67
Gulf Coast, 78
Gull, 23, 34, 40, 48

Habitat: 23, 24, 32, 36;
    dynamics, 51–70;
    management, 84, 85–87, 103
Hawk, marsh, 89
Herbicides, 80, 83, 101
Herbivore, 25, 27, 39, 42, 55, 57, 77–78, 84
Heron, 23, 27, 39, 46
Hovering, 32
Hunting, 75, 100, 103, 108, 120
Hyacinth, water, 22, 80, 102
Hydrilla, 101
Hydrologist, 5, 11
Hydrology, 11–13

Ibis, 23, 33, 39
Ice, 7, 74
Ichthyologist, 5
Illinois, 89
Indian, American, 57
Insecticides, 95, 101
Insects 4, 31, 40, 49, 52, 67, 117
Insolation, 10
Instability (water levels), 70, 100–101
Invertebrates: 36, 38, 41, 45, 47–50, 53, 56,
    68, 70, 73, 82, 84, 101;
    sampling, 53, 117
Iowa, viii, 51, 52, 89, 90, 96, 103
Iraq, 102
Irrigation, 109
Island, 23, 79

Jellyfish, 47

Lake, 9, 10, 58, 70, 82, 96, 98, 100
Lark, 51
Latitude, 51

Layers (strata), 24
Lease, 120
Leech, 113
Level ditching, 79
Life support, 92
Lily, 56, 98
Limnology, 5, 116
Livestock, 28, 74, 77, 101
Locomotion, 32
Loon, 36, 37, 53
Louisiana, 52, 95, 111

Mammals, 5, 39, 41–44, 52, 118
Management, marsh, viii, 71–87, 100, 119, 120
Manitoba, 9, 87, 95
Map, cover, 113
Marsh:
    acquisition, 73;
    classification, 13–15;
    coastal, 17;
    conservation, 71, 79, 108–110;
    creation, 82;
    deterioration, 101;
    diversity, 17, 71, 73;
    emergent, 3;
    formation, 7;
    future, 107–111;
    hydrology, 11–13;
    losses, 88–90, 108–110;
    restoration, 81–82;
    riverine, 10, 46;
    saline, 12;
    study techniques, 113–118;
    tidal, 4;
    values, 88–93
Mayfly, 48
Meadow, 20, 47, 77, 119, 120
Meadowlark, 66
Merganser, 28, 33
Methiocarb, 96
Mice, 26, 35, 44, 58, 118
Michigan, 89
Midge (Chironomid), 33, 34, 47, 48
Midwest, 103
Millet, 119
Mink, 23, 35, 43, 46, 58, 98
Minnesota, 51, 89, 95, 102, 103
Minnow, 45, 47, 118
Mitigation, 82, 110
Model, 68, 92

Mollusks, 33, 49
Mosquitoes, 31, 47, 95, 98, 117
Moss, 13
Mud, 58, 75, 114, 118
Muskrat: 11, 19, 23, 26, 42–44, 52, 55, 58–
    62, 64, 68, 70, 74–77, 90, 95, 98, 100,
    103, 114, 118, 120–121;
    round-tailed, 42
Mustelid, 44

National Audubon Society, 112
National Park Service, 107
Nature Conservancy, 73, 112
Nature study center, 102
Negative aspects (of marshes), 93–96
Net, butterfly, 117
Niche, 32, 85
Nitrogen, 26, 28, 29, 70, 102
North Central, 78
North Dakota, 51, 73, 89
Northwest Territory (Canada), 104
Nutria, 42, 55, 77, 103, 121
Nutrient, viii, 9, 18, 23, 28–30, 56, 70, 74,
    78, 83, 89, 100–101, 104

Oats, 95
Ohio, 103
Oligotrophy, 28, 53
Omnivore, 25, 27, 37, 84
Oriole, 24
Ornithologist, 5
Otter, 23, 42
Owl, 51
Oxygen, 45, 92

Pampas, 42
Pelican, 46
Permafrost, 10
Permit (to modify wetlands), 109
pH, 116
Phase, vegetation, 15
Pheasant, 51, 66
Phosphorus, 26, 28–30, 70
Pike, 45
Plankton: 49, 70;
    sampling, 102, 117
Plants:
    aquatic, 101;
    buoyancy, 19, 52, 57;

community, 100;
    dominant, 10;
    emergent, 21, 45;
    floating, 22, 30;
    floating-leaf, 21;
    growth, 56;
    life form, 18, 19, 81, 115, 116;
    line-intercept, 115;
    nuisance, 80;
    rootstocks, 42, 55, 58;
    sampling, 114–116;
    seeds, 75;
    species composition, 57, 58, 89;
    structure, viii, 20–24;
    submergent, 21, 45, 57, 76, 120;
    tubers, 32, 42, 57, 75;
    water tolerance, 19, 56–57;
Platform, floating, 81
Pleistocene, 7
Policy, 108, 110, 111
Politics, 111
Pollutants, 29, 50
Polygonal earth, 10
Pondweed (*Potamogeton* spp.), 22, 39, 56,
    57, 119
Pool, 24, 43, 118
Population, viii, 104, 111
Potassium, 28
Pothole:
    artificial, 79;
    blasted, 79;
    glacial prairie, 7, 12, 42, 73, 78, 89, 96
Precipitation, 11, 51, 108
Predator, 23, 45, 46
Producer, 25
Production, 4, 29
Protozoa, 26, 31, 47, 49
Ptarmigan, 51

Raccoon, 23, 35, 44, 46
Rail, 24, 34, 40, 103, 104, 119, 121
Reed, 13, 29, 35, 58, 102
Relict, 104
Reptile, 46, 47, 118
Research, 4, 55, 87, 90, 101, 111, 113
Resource segregation, 32, 33
Rice, 95
River: 9, 50;
    delta, 10
Roads, 95

Rodents, 58
Role (ecological), 25, 36
Runoff, 12

Salamander, 45, 53
Sampling, 114
Sandpiper, 78
Science, 104, 110
Scientific names, 122–124
Scuds (sideswimmers), 49
Seal, 11
Seasonality, 28, 51–53
Section 404, 109
Sedge, 3, 21, 29, 32, 56
Seed dispersal, 81, 82
Seral, 53
Sewage 101
Shorebirds, 77
Shoveler, 39, 70
Shredder, 26, 50
Shrew, 44
Shrimp, fairy, 49
Sideswimmers (scuds), 49
Siltation, 10, 109
Skiing, 98, 108, 114
Skunk, 35
Smartweed, 119
Snail, 33, 49, 70
Snake, 39, 46
Snipe, 103, 118, 121
Snow, 9, 11, 108, 114
Sociobiology, 104
Soil, 7, 28, 56, 95
Soil Conservation Service, 108
Sounds, animal, 34
South Dakota, 89
Sowbug, 49
Sparrow, 35, 37, 66
Spawn, 18, 45
Species associations, 36
Species diversity, 5, 101
Species richness, 5, 32
Sponge, 47
Squirrel, 35
Stickleback, 45
Sticky-trap, 117
Stork, 39
Strata (layers), 24
Stream flow, 74
Substrate, 18

Succession, 53–58, 85, 101
Sunflowers, 95
Swallows, 35, 48
Swamp, 14, 46, 47, 88
Swan, 39, 89, 104
Sweden, 102
Swimmer's itch, 113

Teal, blue-winged, 33, 35, 38, 70, 90
Tern, 23, 34, 40, 48, 64, 98
Texas, 95, 104
Threatened species, 103–104
Tiles, 81, 88, 95
Toad, 34, 45, 46, 104
Transpiration, 12
Trapping, 75, 77, 108
Trout, 84
Tundra, 44, 51
Turbidity, 45, 116
Turtle, 46, 56

United States, 89, 91, 102, 103

Valuation (marsh), 88–93
Vegetation:
    change and wildlife, 62–67;
    cover-water ratio, 73, 79;
    diversity, 72;
    management, 76, 77;
    natural change, 74;
    structure, 20–24;
    wildlife-induced change, 54

Waders, 77
Walkway, 102
Water, vii, 12, 13, 18–20, 24, 42, 52, 55, 57,
    70, 74, 75, 77, 82, 96–102, 107–108, 119–121
Water Bank Program, 108, 111
Waterbirds, 4, 79
Water control, 120
Water-crowfoot, 22
Water fleas, 49
Waterfowl, 32, 73, 78, 100, 103
Watermeal, 30
Water purification, 101–102
Water weeds, 83
Weasel, 44, 108, 114
Webbed feet, 26
Weed banks, 93
Wheat, 95

Whitetop (grass), 21
Wigeon, 39
Wilderness, 107
Wildlife, 100
Wildlife biologist, 5
Wildlife harvest, 103
Wildlife resources, 71
Wildlife surplus, 103
Wildlife takers, 103

Wildlife watchers, 102, 103
Willow, 43, 56, 120
Wind, 52
Wisconsin, 88, 92, 95, 103
Wren, 32, 33, 37, 41

Yellowthroat, 35, 41

Zooplankton, 26

Milton W. Weller, formerly head of the department of entomology, fisheries, and wildlife at the University of Minnesota, now is Kleberg Professor of Wildlife Ecology at Texas A & M University. He has studied wetlands and their associated wildlife communities in many parts of the world and is the author of a recently published book on the subject, *The Island Waterfowl.*